Living the Gospel

Living the Gospel

DAVID HOPE

Foreword by Lord Runcie

DARTON·LONGMAN+TODD

First published in 1993 by
Darton, Longman and Todd Ltd
1 Spencer Court
140–142 Wandsworth High Street
London SW18 4JJ

ISBN 0–232–52017–8

A catalogue record for this book is available
from the British Library

Cover: photograph by Ian Jones; design by Jeremy Dixon

Phototypeset by Intype, London
Printed and bound in Great Britain
at the University Press, Cambridge

Contents

CHURCH AND MISSION

Foreword

In these sermons and other writings, David Hope shows us a good deal of himself. To be Bishop of London at the present moment is to engage with the Church of England at its most diverse – some would say its most divisive. Bishop David reveals himself as sensitive to particular issues, and determined to encourage and support everyone in his diocese. He has no illusions about the difficulty of his task.

One theme that runs through this book is the need to keep talking in the midst of disagreement. One of Bishop David's favourite words is 'courtesy'. No theology can be taken seriously which does not include respect for other people, however much their views differ from one's own.

Another theme is the refusal to equate size with importance. Small can be beautiful. Indeed, an effective ministry to the poor, the weak, the apparently insignificant will often look small if it remains human and personal.

A third strand in these writings echoes St Paul's conviction that God accepts us as we are. We do not have to earn God's love. 'Freely you have received: freely give.' Those Pauline words illustrate the imperative for moral discipline in the body of Christ.

The Church is nourished by word and sacrament. Bishop David stresses the centrality of the eucharist, yet warns that the eucharist must never become an end in itself. Christ feeds us that we may feed others – not least the poor, the weak, the apparently insignificant.

I detect a holy impatience with what Bishop David sees as wrong priorities. 'Often there is much talking, far too little action.' What we say matters less than who we are. There is no support here for any inverted parochialism, any spirit of self-satisfied congregationalism. Instead, there is a constant demand for integrity, for co-operation, and for visible signs of the faith we profess.

The Church of England knows David Hope as a bishop uneasy about the ordination of women, and about the legislation now coming into being. He has sat on every committee. He knows every argument, and sees every pitfall. He does not, as yet, see his own way forward with clarity. That is hardly to be wondered at. He sets out some of the options he must face in the immediate future, and lets us see something of the process by which he is feeling his way.

David Hope is a man well named. This book shows him as a bishop of integrity, of pastoral sensitivity, of courage and toughness, but above all of hope – hope rooted and grounded in the good news of Jesus Christ. Here is a bishop not afraid to acknowledge that sometimes there are no easy answers to hard questions, that obedience can require living with uncertainty. But here too is a man confident that with patience – and courtesy – we may indeed hope to discern and do God's will.

Introduction

I have made no secret of the fact that the decision to accept the See of London was one of the most difficult decisions I have ever had to make. From much that had been said and written, the whole enterprise seemed impossible. The outlook was distinctly gloomy. Yet having now completed extended visits to every deanery together with a wide and varied range of other establishments and institutions, I am aware of the tremendous riches and resources available. I am also aware of so much which is positive about the mission of the Church in this large and complex diocese.

My hope is that this collection of sermons, addresses and one or two specially written chapters, will give the flavour of what I have been about as I have sought to bring some shape and direction to the diocese as a whole.

Obviously one of the major areas dominating the life of the Church continues to be the ordination of women to the ministerial priesthood. I have attempted to share as honestly and openly as I can something of my own views, and how I have tried to approach this subject in a diocese where polarised opinions about this, as about other matters, are very evident. There is a deep inner and personal conflict between one's own conscientiously held views and convictions, and the exercising of an episcopal ministry as a focus of unity for all. The result of the vote is now known, yet the process of charting a way ahead and forward continues.

It is very easy, I believe, to be deflected from the main thrust of the Church's purpose which must surely be mission. It is this overwhelming priority to which the Church is called in this as in every age, and I have been keen for the diocese to respond with vigour to the Saviour's call to 'go and make disciples'. Further, the deepening of the spiritual roots of the Anglican tradition and inheritance remain an important priority for all, for without the risk of the contemplative dimension the Church will inevitably succumb to the prevailing superficiality of materialism and consumerism. We are not called to be conformed to the ways of this world but rather to be 'transformed by the renewal of your mind that you may prove what is the will of God, what is good and acceptable and perfect' (Romans 12:2).

Finally, I am enormously grateful to those who in the first place suggested that I should consider the possibility of such a book as this and in particular to the very considerable help and assistance of the staff at London House, the Revd Rob Marshall, Diocesan Communications Officer, and Morag Reeve of Darton, Longman and Todd, without whom it simply would not have been possible.

THE CHRISTIAN JOURNEY

1

Conversion*

Now as he journeyed he approached Damascus, and suddenly a light from heaven flashed about him. (Acts 9:3)

Of the many bible stories told to us as children the conversion of St Paul still sticks in my mind as one of the most exciting and dramatic. Paul had set out from Jerusalem to Damascus with one intention only: 'still breathing threats to slaughter the Lord's disciples.' But on the way he experiences a dramatic conversion – he sees a light from heaven, he falls to the ground and he hears a voice. The purpose of his journey is radically changed. No longer is he set against the Lord's disciples, rather he journeys on to join them.

Since then many people have been willing and ready to spring to their feet in order to give testimony about their conversion – that moment, that time, that place when they met the Lord face to face and experienced a change in the direction of their lives. Equally there have always been very many people in the Church who cannot point to such a conversion moment and may therefore feel somewhat second-rate, perhaps even cheated because they have not had so spectacular an experience. That does not mean to say, however, that they have not had a conversion experience. I would suggest that, for this latter group, their conversion experience has taken a somewhat different route – the route of the unspectacular, a route which has been more a questioning, a gradual growing and deepening in the Christian faith and life. Conversion is, I believe, neither just or only 'event', nor is it just or only 'process'. It is both, and for any Christian

*St Paul's Covent Garden, Sunday 26 January 1992

person baptism, that sacramental moment of dying with Christ and rising to new life, is the outward and visible sign of the inward and spiritual reality of conversion. It is the sign of the action of God towards us and upon us – that seed of faith, hope and love implanted in us once upon a time but which has yet to sprout, blossom and flourish. So it is true to say that our Christian life day by day is all about conversion. Conversion is an aspect of our faith and life which is as much for today and tomorrow as it is for testimony about 'once upon a time'.

So what are the implications for us of this process of conversion? It is perfectly clear from Paul's own writings that even though the Damascus Road event was for him so striking and life-changing, he nevertheless had to face the fact that he also had to undergo much growing and maturing into the person the Lord would have him be, and any growth involves some degree of struggle and change. One of Paul's major themes is about growing into Christ, putting on Christ, being holy. It is the call to sanctification and holiness of life – ensuring that the foundation and framework for Christ-like life is firmly secured inwardly and that the fruits of that inwardness are displayed outwardly in our dealings and relationships with each other; indeed with everyone we meet.

This holiness of life – the call to sanctification – is well set out every time we come together, wherever we may be, for holy communion. And perhaps it is not too difficult in the context of church and congregation at worship to recognise the fact that we are a holy fellowship. We come side by side at holy communion as members one of another, each in our own human need, frailty and brokenness, just as we are. It is the risen Lord who greets us; we receive the bread of life and the cup of the new covenant – the sacramental signs of his abiding presence with us and within us as we go forth on our various ways. Yet even as we go, we need to be attentive to the things of God. The world, the daily round – whatever that may be – is always in danger of taking us over and running us. It is our business to ensure we find some time, however brief, for daily prayer, some space for a reflective reading of the Word of God, that Word which is a light unto our feet and a lantern unto our path, so that in the thick of things we do not lose our bearings. Outwardly we may be very busy, very absorbed, we may be fed up, bored; yet inwardly the process of conversion continues. The 'outwardness' of holiness is not a miserable begrudging piety or a greater religiosity; rather it is an altogether deeper engagement in life and living with all the risks and precariousness that that involves but with a certain and cheerful faith that God does actually have the whole world in his hands.

It is precisely this risk and precariousness which we see so clearly lived out in Paul's subsequent ventures – his missionary journeys. In spite of everything there is an over-riding optimism and confidence in the Lord who has so transformed his life. Just think for a moment of what he endured in his journeying. He speaks movingly and with feeling about frequent imprisonment, flogging and beatings; he speaks of danger from the sword and from wild beasts, nakedness and hunger, shipwreck and so on. And yet there is an equally strong theme of continual prayer, of rejoicing in the Lord. The experience of our own journeying may not be a literal shipwreck, may not be an actual beating or flogging; nevertheless the ups and downs of our lives can leave us feeling somewhat battered.

The example and pattern of the Apostle Paul is one of cheerfulness, faithfulness and perseverance. These are some of the ingredients which move us towards that holiness of life which I mentioned earlier. Further, when there are so many distractions around us in a whole variety of ways, our job is, in a spirit of cheerfulness, faithfulness and perseverance, to keep our eyes fixed on Jesus. He is the author and finisher of our faith, who for the joy which was set before him despised the shame and is now sat down at the right hand of the throne of God. This is the basic truth to which every parish is called and committed; in the working at it and the living of it we follow in the way of the Lord Jesus Christ so that others will find it possible to follow in the same way also. For at the heart of any missionary strategy is the deep renewal of heart and life.

At the end of every eucharist we are bidden to go forth . . . to love and serve the Lord. We can go forth with a song of joy in our hearts and a word of hope on our lips, certain and confident that he, in whose name we have gathered together and who has nourished us in word and sacrament, is the faithful one; he has committed himself to be with us not only in the here and now but also in our going forth and into the future. Furthermore, it is a going forth in love, a love of which Paul himself so rhapsodises in that famous passage in 1 Corinthians 13 – a love which is patient and kind, not zealous or boastful, not arrogant or rude; a love which does not rejoice at wrong but rejoices in the right. In short, a love which bears all things, believes all things, hopes all things, endures all things. It is in the strength and power of this love of the Lord that we dare to go forth into the world, so that abiding and living in this love not only we but many more people will come in the spirit of the same love to conversion, to a living and lively faith in the risen Lord and Saviour Jesus Christ.

2

Strength in Weakness*

Judah was the father of Perez and Zerah by Tamar . . . Salmon was the father of Boaz by Rahab, and Boaz the father of Obed by Ruth . . . And David was the father of Solomon by the wife of Uriah. (Matthew 1:3–6)

In Cranmer's great collect for the Second Sunday in Advent, we are exhorted to read, mark, learn and inwardly digest the scriptures – the writings both of Old and New Testaments which were finally settled as the canon of scripture by the late fourth century, although the bulk of the collection had been agreed much earlier.

One of the reasons why it took so long to reach agreement as to what should be in, and what should be out, was the nature and the tone of some of the disputed texts. Indeed, to some extent the argument which began in those early years has continued unabated to the present; for ever since there have been those who would argue that this or that passage, this book or that book, ought not to form a part of the Word of God for our time. I suppose one of the most radical of such views was expressed by Marcion in the late second century. He rejected the whole of the Old Testament and much of the New Testament besides on the grounds that they offended his views about the God of love whom we find in Jesus. He believed Paul alone, apart from his pastoral epistles, had got things just right. I suppose that today many would have considerable sympathy with Marcion and his followers.

Indeed, individual laity and clergy pick and choose, and it is with all this in mind that I would like to concentrate on

*St James's Piccadilly, Sunday 8 December 1991

one particular passage of scripture, studiously avoided by the compilers of more recent Anglican lectionaries, but which I believe to be absolutely crucial and vital. The passage to which I refer is the opening sixteen verses of St Matthew's Gospel – Jesus' pedigree. It looks tedious and reads boringly if not ridiculously. Yet, to excise this passage from the Gospel is to excise an indispensable part of what Matthew's Gospel, and the whole gospel message, is about.

So why should we bother ourselves at all with this canine-like fictional pedigree with regard to Jesus? Why plough through the names of Abraham the father of Isaac, Isaac the father of Jacob . . . Jehoshaphat father of Joram and Joram the father of Uzziah . . . simply in order to get to verse sixteen – 'and Jacob the father of Joseph the husband of Mary of whom Jesus was born, who is called Christ'. Why plough through this tedious and apparently irrelevant list of names in order to get to verse sixteen which is the real point of the whole passage?

I would like to suggest that embedded within these sixteen verses are four names, the names of four women in fact, Tamar, Rahab, Ruth and Bathsheba, which give us the clue to the main purpose of the whole passage. But yet, could not the compiler have sought out four rather more improving names than these? Or do we have here perhaps a clear example of what the feminist writers would call 'we told you so'? An example of the strongly patriarchal background of biblical writing which seeks only to do down women, hence the choice of these four?

So why are women mentioned at all in these sixteen verses, and why these four particular women? I hope I might be able to point us in a rather more positive direction, a direction which is central to the good news Jesus brings. Let us examine then the possibilities before us.

The first and most obvious view is that here we have four well-known 'sinners' whose inclusion at this early point in Matthew's Gospel foreshadows for Matthew's readers the role of Jesus as the Saviour of sinful humanity. There might even be a cryptic form of apologetic against certain Jewish claims that Mary herself was an adulteress who had conceived Jesus as the fruit of a sinful relationship. But I am not sure that the immediate identification of these four as 'sinners' can necessarily or easily be sustained. In fact Jewish piety of Jesus' time lets them off pretty lightly. Tamar was esteemed as a saintly Jewish proselyte, a converted Canaanite, and it was by her initiative that the family line of Judah's son, her deceased husband, had been perpetuated. Rahab, prostitute as she was, was also a proselyte. Indeed she was a heroine for having assisted Israel at Jericho. Hebrews 11:31 makes her a model of faith! Did Ruth really sin with Boaz? The Old Testament is neither clear nor explicit. And in view of Solomon's birth and subsequent reign, Bathsheba's adultery is not always condemned in the rabbinic literature in the strident terms you might expect. So I believe there are very good grounds for suggesting that the label 'sinners' or 'condemned' would hardly have sprung immediately to the minds of Matthew's readers.

A second possibility, favoured by Luther, and which has a good deal more to commend it, is that the four women were regarded as 'foreigners'. Again they are included here by way of a prelude to a major theme taken up by Matthew throughout his Gospel, that Jesus, yes, Son of David, the Jewish Messiah, was related by ancestry also to Gentiles. Jesus is both Son of David and Son of Abraham, a far more inclusive title which is picked up and reflected in the journey of the Magi in Chapter 2. As we have already seen, Tamar and Rahab were originally Canaanite, Ruth a Moabite and Bathsheba, whilst not identified as a foreigner as such, is nevertheless referred to as wife of Uriah the Hittite. Yet I am not sure that this explanation is necessarily along the right lines, for both Tamar and Rahab were much more regarded as converts than they were as foreigners. So there is no real consistency for all four if we pursue the argument in this way.

Thus far, however, we have not considered at all the fifth woman who is mentioned in these verses, namely 'Mary of whom Jesus was born, who is called Christ'. Is not the real answer to our search for some coherent reason as to why these names are included at this point to be found in including Mary in the list rather than excluding her? If so, what, we must ask, does this lead us to think of Matthew's purposes?

I would suggest that there are two elements in the birth of

Jesus which combine to draw in the mention of the other four
women, elements which all five have in common. Firstly,
there is something extraordinary or irregular in their union
with their partners, a union which, though it may have been
scandalous to outsiders, nevertheless is part and parcel of the
lineage of the Messiah. Secondly, each of the women shared
an initiative or played an important part in God's plan, and
so came to be considered the instrument of God's purpose,
of God's Holy Spirit. Indeed do not all five of them demon-
strate very amply how God so often uses the unexpected to
triumph over human obstacles and intervenes on behalf of
his planned Messiah? It is this combination then of the
scandalous or irregular union and of divine intervention
through the particular woman that explains best Matthew's
choice of women for inclusion in his genealogy.

So, far from being dismissive of the role of women, here is
Matthew highlighting in his list of the high and the mighty
men the reality that it was these women who were just as
much the significant persons in God's plan towards the salvation of the world.

Yet, there is more, I believe, which springs out of these
sixteen verses and which is very pertinent for the Church in
every age, not least our own.

The first thing is that God takes us just as we are: no
matter what mess we may have got ourselves into, no matter
how grim things may seem to be, there God is, with us,
alongside us, ready and waiting to turn our despair about
ourselves into hope. Indeed I am reminded of some words of
another very significant woman, very influential both in her
time and subsequently. St Teresa of Avila's prayer concerning
herself was this, 'that however useless and hopeless I may
seem to be I will never cease to praise you O my God for
having made me just as I am'. The difficulty is that so many
of us do spend much of our time, energy and effort in self-
rejection rather than looking to the enormous possibilities and
potentialities that God can make even out of what can so
often feel like a total disaster and complete failure. The words
of a well-known Advent hymn set out this major theme of
good news about the Lord's coming to us as we are, where
we are: 'He comes the broken heart to bind, the bleeding soul

to cure, and with the treasures of his grace, enrich the humble poor.' So there is the clear message that while some of us may be tempted to give up on ourselves, God never does. He longs for us to be the attractive and beautiful people he has created us to be.

A second, and not entirely unrelated, theme, is that of God's power being made perfect in our human weakness – and that goes for all of us, men just as much as women. It is a call to let go of that arrogance and pride which lurks in every human being; to acknowledge that much as we may wish to secure control and power both over ourselves and others, this in the end will only lead to a diminishment and a further disfiguring of the image of God in us and in our neighbour. Rather we are called to ensure the more that we are controlled by the power of God's Spirit, where love is drained in making full, bound in setting others free, poor in making many rich, weak in giving power to be. In this way our weaknesses, our very vulnerability, frailty and failure, become our greatest strength in ensuring God's will and purposes both for us and for every human being.

On the face of it, then, these sixteen verses from St Matthew's Gospel are a boring irrelevance to be struck out, but with greater attention and further reflection they bring forth a pearl of great price. They speak to us of *the* truth of the Incarnation, God with us, God among us, still, always, everywhere, even to the end of all things. And now to round it all off with a poem sent to me by a correspondent:

TAMAR

Exceedingly odd
Is the means by which God
Has provided our path to the heavenly shore:
Of the girls from whose line
The true light was to shine
There was one an adulteress, one was a whore.

There was Tamar who bore—
What we all should deplore—
A fine pair of twins to her father-in-law;

And Rahab the harlot,
Her sins were as scarlet,
As red as the thread which she hung from the door,

Yet alone of her nation
She came to Salvation
And lived to be mother of Boaz, of yore.
And he married Ruth,
A gentile uncouth
In a manner quite counter to Biblical lore;

And from her there did spring
Blessed David the King,
Who walked on his palace one evening, and saw
The wife of Uriah,
From whom he did sire
A baby that died—oh and princes a score.

And a mother unmarried
It was, too, that carried
God's Son, who was laid in a cradle of straw,
That the moral might wait
At the heavenly gate
While the sinners and publicans go in before,
Who have not earned their place,
But received it by grace
And have found them a righteousness not of the Law.

3

Discipleship*

To be a light to lighten the Gentiles and to be the glory of thy people Israel. (Luke 2:32)

One of my favourite places is the east coast of Yorkshire, Flamborough Head to be precise. It can be wild and stormy; it can be serene and picturesque. The cliffs are both precipitous and majestic. If you want plenty of fresh air, then a long walk on the cliff tops is always rejuvenating. One of the features on the exposed cliff top is a lighthouse, and nearby is a disused beacon tower which preceded the lighthouse in earlier times. In the darkness of the night, the beacon of light can be seen for a very great distance both by land and sea. It is a guiding light, a sign to the traveller which brings security, a light which enables you to get your bearings and to keep them.

Light is a strong theme in the Gospels – Jesus Christ the light of the world, the light which ever shines in the darkness of this world's night but which the darkness can never or will never overcome.

The account of the Presentation in the Temple is poignant and moving. When the customs of the law have been observed, we see the old man Simeon taking into his arms the young child Jesus and uttering those words which, from the very earliest of times, have formed the evening hymn of the universal Church, the Nunc Dimittis. They are words of joyful confidence and of peaceful resignation. It is no wonder that they have often formed the struggling prayerful words of those who have been in the process of dying. For Simeon,

*The Grosvenor Chapel, Sunday 2 February 1992

with this child in his arms, dying is now less of a fearful unknown and more of a joyful hope and expectation. For like all Israel he has been waiting for a very long time to set eyes upon the Lord's Christ. Now that waiting has been fulfilled and he can die a happy and contented man.

To be a light to lighten the Gentiles and to be the glory of thy people Israel.

What then may we glean from reflecting on this narrative of St Luke? The first thing I would suggest comes from the simple and straightforward observance by Jesus' parents, Joseph and Mary, of the law's demands. Does this not highlight for us the continuing need for the discipline and framework of commitment to our being in the Lord's house on the Lord's day around the Lord's table week by week? In so doing we are one with our brothers and sisters in Christ, not only in Britain but throughout the rest of the world; indeed we are one with Christian believers from the very beginning. Sunday – the first day of the week – is special. It is *the* day when we come together for worship, to celebrate that mighty act of God in raising Jesus from the dead and bringing him to glory. And it is in the holy and saving mysteries of word and sacrament that we are drawn into the movement of Christ's own self-offering to the Father. But we are, of course, human, and church-going can become tedious and dull; we may feel we are getting little out of it; there are a hundred and one reasons why from time to time our commitment may falter – indeed why we stop going altogether. The Lukean narrative of the Presentation of Our Lord sets before us the dedicated devotion of Simeon and Anna, of Mary and Joseph, in their quiet, unobtrusive and persistent commitment to their religious duties. This acts as a timely reminder to each of us of the need to make a priority of our commitment both to public worship and, in public worship, to each other. If we are not careful our busy schedules can take us over and dictate the priorities of our lives and living.

Perhaps it is here that a second theme emerges – namely that of waiting. Most of the waiting I do, I must confess, is what I would call frustrating waiting – for a tube, for a bus, at a bank, in a supermarket – when the waiting seems to go on and on, and inside I feel myself beginning to reach boiling point. In contrast, Simeon's waiting is generous and expectant; and I suspect we need to heed something of this for the good of our own souls and lives as well as for the good and well-being of our society. Perhaps our prayer needs to be more about stopping, looking and listening; remember the words of the psalmist: 'be still and know that I am God.' Of course, it is much more easily said than done to let go and let God; to release that turmoil of things within, to hand them over, to cast all our cares upon the Lord and to go on our way rejoicing. Nevertheless it is a necessary dimension for Christian discipleship today.

So how does this aspect of the tradition impinge on our life and lifestyle? Where are our moments of waiting? Where is the space on a regularly recurring basis? Is there a time for retreat and renewal? When, in the words of Isaac the Syrian, can we 'dive deep within ourselves thereby discovering the rungs by which to ascend'? When can we seek the kingdom of heaven that is within – in the still centre of our own being? Where are the times when we can be still and know that 'I am God', be attentive to the discipline of prayer day by day, to the regular reading of and reflection upon the holy scriptures, to ensuring that we have that space and silence in our inner-most being so that the noisy cacophony of the world can still be pierced and challenged by the Word of God which is 'sharper than a two-edged sword piercing to the division of soul and spirit . . . and discerning the thoughts and intentions of the heart'?

To be a light to lighten the Gentiles and to be the glory of thy people Israel.

The Feast of Light is a sign and symbol of the destiny to which we are called and which we await: yet in which we already share as with angels and archangels and all the company of heaven we hear on the distant ear the triumph song of heaven, we catch a glimpse of God's glory. This is what the worship of the Church is most fundamentally about; it is not entertainment, nor is it drama or a concert or anything else. It is the celebration in word and sacrament of the fact that the kingdom of heaven has drawn near; that God's king-

dom has come on earth as it is in heaven and that as we
share in holy communion we have a share in that sacred
banquet wherein Christ is received, the memory of his death
and resurrection renewed and a pledge of future glory given
us.

This is good news indeed – but good news which we cannot
and dare not keep for ourselves. The same Lord, whom we
celebrate as light of the world, bids us: 'Let your light so
shine among men that they may see your good works and
give glory to your Father in heaven' (Matthew 5:16). In other
words, it is our business to be as lights – beacons like that
lighthouse with which I began, whereby others may discern
and recognise something of the light, life and joy of the Lord
Jesus Christ. It is the summons, to use the words of one of
the prayers after communion, for us who share Christ's body
to live his risen life; we who drink his cup to bring life to
others; we whom the Spirit lights to give light to the world.
This is expressed in the dismissal at the conclusion of every
eucharist: 'go in peace to love and serve the Lord.' It is the
imperative to be as lights on Monday, Tuesday and as the
week goes on – yes, even when our patience is getting to
breaking point; when things do not turn out the way we
expect them to; when other people are quite impossible. It is
the commitment on our part to muster those deep down
energies in the pursuit of patience and kindness; of long-
suffering and gentleness; of thinking the best rather than the
worst – in short, to realise more fully and more actively those
gifts of the Spirit which are renewed in us as we share together
the bread of life and the cup of the new covenant.

There is no slick or easy way for the Christian disciple; we
shall fail and fail often. But the wonder of it is that he loves
us still. Indeed it is just as we are in our frailty, our weakness
and our need of him and of each other that he enfolds us
afresh in his love, that he nourishes us with the bread from
heaven, that he sends us out refreshed and renewed, ourselves
to be the good news of the kingdom of heaven. In the words
of St Augustine of Hippo: 'if you live good lives you yourself
are the Song of new life.'

4

Thankfulness*

And whatever you do, in word or deed, do everything in the name of the Lord Jesus, giving thanks to God the Father through him. (Colossians 3:17)

One of the lessons I learnt early in life was the importance of saying, 'thank you'. There was never a birthday or a Christmas allowed to pass in our house without my parents insisting that my sister and I sat down and wrote 'thank you' letters for the gifts and presents we had received. I have to confess that I did not always obey with a glad and generous heart as I would far sooner have been playing with the toy train or Matchbox car that I had been given. But I am pleased that my parents persevered and taught me a fundamental courtesy.

But 'thank yous' are not just reserved for childhood. We find ourselves using the phrase on all manner of occasions, and there are many situations when 'thank you' is the only appropriate response and is in fact all that can be said – but in saying that one phrase we are saying a great deal more besides.

If we consider that magisterial record of God's dealings with his people as set out for us in the pages of the bible, there is no doubt that thanksgiving is a key element in both Old and New Testaments. Throughout the long and, at times, turbulent history of God's people in the Old Testament – in the bad times, in the difficult times; when they found themselves up against it, when they thought God had forsaken or forgotten them; indeed, when they themselves had more often

*The Chapel Royal, St James's Palace, Sunday 26 July 1992

than not forgotten and forsaken their God; just as much as
in the good, positive and harmonious times – there is always
the underlying theme of thanksgiving to God, perhaps best
typified by the psalmist: 'I will magnify thee O God my King
– I will praise thy name for ever and ever. Every day will I
give thanks unto thee and praise thy name for ever and ever'
(Psalm 145:1–2).

This theme of daily praise of God is reflected just as
strongly in the New Testament. The Apostle Paul at many
points in his letters to those early Christian communities in
Rome, Corinth, Ephesus and Philippi, urges his brothers and
sisters in the Lord to give thanks continuously, unceasingly,
always rejoicing in God.

But Paul was only echoing what was at the very heart of
Jesus' own life and living. As a faithful observer of the Jewish
prayer tradition in which he had been nurtured and to which
he was loyal, Jesus would have paused to give thanks to God,
creator and Lord of the universe, at all times and in all places
– on rising, on washing, on setting out, before a meal, before
retiring to bed; every day punctuated with praise and thanksgiving Godward. There have been very many Christians down
the ages who have taken up this theme and have made it very
evident in their lives, even in the most arduous and terrible
of circumstances.

Further, there is thanksgiving in relation to each other, for
each of us reflects a bit of God's unique and distinctive
creating and fashioning. We may not always like what we see
in the person next door to us, but the Christian message is
that we are to thank God for the gift which he makes to us
of each other. So instead of spending too much energy in a
negatively critical direction, which it is very easy for us to
do, we are encouraged to direct that energy into the rather
more positive enterprise of encouraging, supporting and sustaining each other, and so enhancing the common good – the
life and well-being of the whole community.

We tend to think that such attitudes and expressions of
praise and thanksgiving are all very well if life is going swim-
mingly, if all is indeed well with me and my world. However,
most of us would be very hard pushed indeed to sustain such
an intensity and constancy of praise and thanksgiving. Life

is not one long party. There are disappointments, setbacks and frustrations for all of us, indeed there are times of deep desolation and despair. What then? Is it realistic to be speaking of thanksgiving unceasingly in such circumstances?

I would want to suggest that it is. Indeed I have already hinted at this aspect of thanksgiving in times of adversity, difficulty and trial, and it is very much a part of the New Testament record. My text at the head of the chapter is taken from St Paul's letter to the Christians at Colossae. We can recall how Paul in other parts of his writings sets out for us all that he has endured for the sake of the gospel – hunger and shipwreck, floggings and imprisonment, nakedness and exhaustion – and yet he never goes on about how terrible it all is; quite extraordinarily he urges his fellow believers to 'rejoice in the Lord always and again I say rejoice' (Philippians 4:4).

And whatever you do, in word or deed, do everything in the name of the Lord Jesus, giving thanks to God the Father through him.

When I have joined Christian groups and churches in Africa for worship, I have seen a real sparkle in the eye and smile on the face, in spite of everything. Recently I made a visit to Romania, a country which I had not visited since I had lived there twenty-five years ago. It was a sad and sorry experience to walk the streets of Bucharest and to see the terrible destruction which had taken place in order to accommodate Nicolae Ceauşescu's megalomaniac building plans. Yet still the churches were full as they had been – all two hundred of them in the capital city. I saw people whose faith had kept them going in those dark and terrible days, a people whose resilience still enabled them to celebrate with real praise and thanksgiving their Christian faith and their Christian belonging one with another in the life of the Church. It is, as Archbishop Michael Ramsey once put it so well, 'the joy and thanksgiving expressed by those who, come what may, are beginning to know God in his beauty and loveliness, and to be exposed to his energies'. It is the thanksgiving and joy of knowing that in spite of all the struggling and the setbacks, in spite of the way things may seem to be at this present time, the victory has been won. Christ is risen. Jesus is Lord.

It was that fervent conviction that fired St James to carry the faith on his missionary journeys, and to witness boldly in a pagan and hostile world. We can wonder what the state of his life might have been the day he met Jesus on the seashore, while he and his brother John and his father Zebedee were mending their nets. His encounter with Christ was to give him such cause for thanksgiving and gratitude that he could leave his old life behind and set out into an unknown world of risk and adventure. James would surely have stayed with the safety and security of his life as a fisherman had not his meeting with the Lord changed and transformed him. So joyfully and wholeheartedly was he given to his discipleship of Jesus that he was to become the first among many to be martyred for the faith, being beheaded by Herod Agrippa in AD 44. Doubtless James, like so many who were to follow him, counted this both a privilege and an honour, indeed something for which to be thankful.

When we celebrate the eucharist we are reminded that the primary focus for all Christian living and discipleship is thanksgiving and rejoicing in the Lord. We lay ourselves and our lives, just as we are, before Christ. There is no possibility of pretence here, for we come before the God to whom all hearts are open, all desires known and from whom no secrets are hidden. The wonder of it is that in holy communion he takes us just as we are, though tossed about with many a conflict, many a doubt, fightings within and fears without. He does not scold and remonstrate with us; rather, he feeds us with the bread of life and the cup of the new covenant, the spiritual food of his most precious body and blood. He sets us on our feet and points us once more in the right direction, thus enabling us to go forth with renewed confidence and hope not only in the generosity of his unending love towards us, but, through that generosity, with renewed confidence and hope in ourselves. My prayer is that after each eucharist we will be able to take something of our celebration and thanksgiving into each day as it comes, for no matter how bad things are there is always, I believe, something for which to say 'thank you'.

If we need a model, then perhaps I can commend the example of this prayer of an eight-year-old child in the north of England. She wrote: 'thank you Lord for the dinner ladies that cook so well and the sheep that keep us very warm when it is very cold and thank you for the cows that give us milk so that we can put it on our cornflakes and thank you very much for my teacher that tells me a very lot of sums and that makes me very very clever. Amen.'

There is a naturalness, straightforwardness, spontaneity and simplicity about this prayer which is much to be admired and followed. It recognises God's generous, loving and sustaining presence with us, within us, among us and around us – at all times and in all places. That is the basic message of the scriptures – it is the basic message for our lives today and every day. We should not be surprised, for it is precisely what the risen Lord and Saviour has promised to us and for us: 'Lo, I am with you always even to the close of the age.' So whatever we do in word or in deed we must do everything in the name of the Lord Jesus Christ, giving thanks to God the Father through him.

5

Small is Beautiful*

And the angel said to them: I bring you good news of a great joy which will come to all the people. (Luke 2:10)

One aspect of Christmas is about keeping in touch, keeping in touch with all kinds of people – our family, our relatives, friends, acquaintances in the present, acquaintances from the past. The once-a-year card of greeting and good wishes is surely a sign which says very powerfully that the bonds, which have at some time or another been forged, always remain in place. It even goes for those with whom we may not be quite so friendly, those with whom we have been at odds at some stage, those with whom there have been, and possibly still are, deep differences; Christmas is a time for throwing out a further line of communication, for gestures suggesting that perhaps things might be better in the future than they have been in the past.

But why do we make such gestures? People say, 'Well, it's the spirit of Christmas'. I don't think we should be too cynically dismissive of the efforts we struggle to make, even in our secularised society, for Christmas at heart is about giving. It is about sharing and generosity; about forgiving and forgetting that which has been, so that we might press on to that which lies before us. The good news which the angels announce with great joyfulness is indeed Emmanuel, God with us; God alongside us and among us; God becoming one of us; God taking upon himself our human nature with all its spots and wrinkles, with all its imperfections, weaknesses and

*The Polytechnic of Central London's Carol Service at All Saints, Margaret Street, Friday 13 December 1991

vulnerabilities. In other words the announcement of the angels is that God takes each one of us seriously. He comes to us and among us just as we are, right where we are. In so doing he longs for us to become the unique, distinctive and beautiful people he has created and wills us to be. The trouble is that so often we simply fail to recognise the good and positive things about ourselves. We can be dismissive and self-rejecting almost to the point of giving up on ourselves. Yet God never does and God never will give up on us.

This good news is lived out and experienced in a great variety of ways, in a wide range of people. When the hostages, Terry Waite, John McCarthy and Jackie Mann, returned to this country from the dark confines of their imprisonment, it was clearly evident that the good news which the angels bring had sustained and upheld them; had enabled them to keep going and to keep their spirits up even in the days of darkest adversity. Their generosity of spirit, their capacity to forgive, had not been quenched even through such dark and wounding experiences.

It is without doubt a fact that bad news is the headline puller. Bad news stories abound among us; they reflect the way in which the fragile nature of our common humanity can so easily be drawn into all that which is worst about ourselves – violence and strife, hatred and division, war and killing. Yet, this always needs to be set in the wider and broader context of the immense possibilities that exist for good – for compassion and care, for love and concern, for mercy and for peace. These possibilities are lived out in the life of the child born in a stable, and we see the first fruits of them clearly at work in the daily lives of so many ordinary people; we see the quiet unsung saint-like qualities which ensure that we are not overcome by evil but show, rather, that it is possible to overcome evil by good.

The good news which is for all people is a message of hope. It is good news that things need not necessarily be the way they are and that each day we have the opportunity to set forth along that new and living way already patterned by Mary's boy child. The tinsel and razzmatazz of Christmas is but froth and it will soon dissipate. Indeed the sadness is that hardly has Christmas Day passed than people begin to say,

'Well, now that Christmas is over . . .'. The truth is that Christmas is not over and will never be over. Whatever the odds may seem to be against us, we need to be striving to ensure that the generosity of the Christmas spirit is not left behind like Christmas past, but is indeed lived out day by day.

The world's ills may appear immense and intractable, and our efforts may seem completely ineffectual, but we should not be deterred. Christmas affirms that our poor efforts are essential if hope for a better world is at all to be entertained. In the helplessness and fragility of a new-born child is God's message that small is beautiful, and, in the words of the prophet Zephaniah: 'a day for small things no doubt but who would dare despise it.' How often it is that in and through small beginnings, massive change has been and continues to be effected. Christmas is God's invitation to us to be with him as he is with us – always, everywhere and eternally – for the shaping of a new world, a world of justice and righteousness, a world of love and peace. This is truly good news for all the people.

6

Hosanna*

Hosanna! Blessed is he who comes in the name of the Lord! Hosanna in the highest! (Mark 11:9–10)

Crowds gather at the drop of a hat. If someone collapses in the street or there is a nasty road accident, people soon gather round, as much out of curiosity as to be of practical help and assistance. Then there are the much larger crowds, the demonstrations – those marching in the pursuit of some cause or other. Hardly a weekend passes in London without a crowd of people gathering in Trafalgar Square or marching down Whitehall to present a petition. There are political meetings and rallies, football matches which draw huge crowds, and all of them have their slogans, their catchwords, their tribal phrases. The chant accompanies the marchers and supporters, keeping before them the purpose of the enterprise for which they are gathered together.

There was a crowd, too, which gathered as Jesus made his way from Bethany, just over the Mount of Olives, to Jerusalem. It was a journey he had often made. But on this day, as the city came into sight across the valley, a group of people gathered round him and very soon a crowd had formed. The sight of him on the donkey riding to Jerusalem had sparked something off in them. Indeed, it sparked off their slogan: 'Hosanna! Blessed is he who comes in the name of the Lord! Hosanna in the highest!' They spread their cloaks in front of him just as they had when Jesu of old was proclaimed king. They cut down and carried palm branches just as they had

---

*The remaining material in this section was first presented on BBC World Service, Lent 1992

when Simon Maccabeus had entered Jerusalem after one of his great victories. They greeted him, too, as a pilgrim, for the familiar phrase, 'Blessed in the name of the Lord is he who comes', was a welcome which they gave to every pilgrim coming to the passover feast. Everywhere the crowd's chant of 'Hosanna' could be heard – a celebration of God's victory and triumph coupled with a longing for liberation; a longing that what God had effected and done in the past, should be effected and done now; a longing for his kingly rule and authority to be ushered in in majestic and stupendous power, the hosts of heaven joining with the hosts on earth to establish his sovereign authority, the kingdoms of this world becoming the kingdoms of our God and of his Christ, a God who will reign for ever and ever.

However, instead of the warrior king on his triumphal steed, we see a man riding on a donkey. There is no weaponry here, no bloodcurdling clamour for death and destruction. The only forces are the crowds which surround him, carrying their palm branches and casting their garments before him. Jesus turns their expectations upside down. He refuses their blandishments to make him a king. Rather, he chooses the way of love, a love which is both human and divine, a love which is prepared to go to the uttermost in self-giving, a love which is made perfect in weakness. But then it all began in the weakness and vulnerability of the cave of Bethlehem with the frailty and fragility of any new-born child. Here is God's Word to us not just then, but for now as well. We are called to lay aside the never-ending struggle for power and domination; to give up the constant wish that we should be something or someone other than the person we actually are; to recognise the fact of our own human limitations; to recognise those areas in us of weakness and vulnerability, and rather than disowning or discarding them seeing in them the potential for transformation and growth. The expectations of others can be encouraging, but they can also be impossible for us. To get it right calls for an altogether deeper faith and trust in the God who was in Christ, and that is a risky business, for there is no telling where it may lead.

7

Journeying

And when he had said this, he went on ahead, going up to Jerusalem.
(Luke 19:28)

Journeys are part and parcel of our lives. Practically every day most of us make a journey. It may simply be from home to a local shop to collect the newspaper, to a post office for stamps, to the local grocer, or it may be something much further afield. Holidays tend to be times when journeys become more daring as we find ourselves part hesitant, part excited, going to new and far off places. For myself I have always enjoyed travel, and even when I go to the same place two or three years running, I always try and vary the route.

There is the place from where we set out, usually our home base, with its certainties and security, a place we know well, where we can relax and be ourselves, somewhere we can sink back into and not have to worry too much about what we wear and what we say – that is home, the starting point.

Then there is the destination. We set out in order to go somewhere, even if it is only a run out in the car. Usually we have some idea of the place we are heading to. There is a fixed point at which we are aiming as we set out, and that is the destination we are heading for, whether we go by the most direct route or wander and meander in a more round-about way.

The bit in between is always much less certain. That is usually where we take a step or two into the unknown. The people we meet, the situation we find ourselves in, the places we get to, are none of them quite planned or in anyway determined beforehand. But I believe that is really what journeys are all about, and even the simplest and shortest of them can throw up something entirely unexpected.

Holy Week is a week when Christians are invited to make a journey. Indeed Jesus says to his disciples, 'Behold we go up to Jerusalem', and it is interesting to note that he does not say 'I' go up to Jerusalem but 'we' go up. Numbers of Christians make the journey quite literally to the Holy Land, as they have done since the very earliest of times. Many more, like myself, make the journey in heart and mind as we move through the special Church services which set before us in music, word and action, in rite and in ceremony, those once upon a time events of the last week of Jesus' life, as we seek to enter more deeply into the mystery of our salvation.

So in the midst of our journeying through life as we reflect upon and are drawn into those saving events of the past, our sights are set firmly forward and to the future, to the joy which is set before us in the risen life of Jesus – his risen life in which even now, through grace, we have a share today. It is this which keeps us going and ensures we are on the right path, for left to ourselves and our own devices and desires, we should be forever going up blind alleys, taking false turnings, finding ourselves going in quite the opposite direction to the one we thought we were heading in. Perhaps that is essentially where some of us find ourselves today, with that sense of having lost our way, unable to find our bearings, listless and directionless, seeming to be going nowhere rather than somewhere. Holy Week and Easter set before us the way and goal of all our journeying, but perhaps much more importantly we are reminded that we never travel alone and that not only has our Lord Jesus Christ gone before us, he is also with us on the way; and he remains with us, even when we have made a mess of things, to set us on the right path and put us in the right direction. We may lose sight and hold of him – he will never lose sight and hold of us.

8

Suffering

And when they came to the place which is called The Skull, there they crucified him, and the criminals, one on the right and one on the left. (Luke 23:33)

Suffering looms large for all of us. Scarcely a day goes by without a news item reporting intense sufferings within the human family, often through conflict, drought, famine and revolution. None of us can ever fail to be moved by the pictures of starving and dying children, but while reports of suffering touch our hearts and lives and provoke us to make some response by way of giving to those agencies seeking to relieve human distress, there is always the sense that such things are distanced from us. Suffering on so huge a scale is difficult to comprehend when we ourselves are not caught up in it.

Yet suffering, to a greater or lesser extent, is the experience of us all, either for ourselves or for others to whom we are close. I find one of the most difficult aspects of pastoral work as a priest and now as bishop is that constant wrestling with the paradox between the God of love I preach about and whom I worship, and the person before me at home or in hospital who has suffered in anguish and pain over many years – a suffering often visible in the body of the person to whom I am ministering.

Recently, I was making an informal pastoral visit to one of the large London hospitals, and I met someone who had been transferred there, together with a friend of hers, for a major operation. The friend had gone down to the theatre three or four days earlier and had not returned – she had died during the operation – and so, added to the woman's suffering, was a grievous anxiety about whether she herself would return or not. I also visited the AIDS ward and met a number of the patients. I did not ask, nor would I have expected to be told, their personal histories. The ravages of the virus were clear to see, so too were the forbearance and courage of the patients as they learned to live each day as it comes and to be thankful.

No doubt all of us, either for ourselves or in another person, have experienced the anguish and pain of human suffering. No doubt we have all cried out, why me? What have I done to deserve this? Where is the God of love, compassion and care in the face of such diminishment?

These are questions which I have often asked in the course of my pastoral work, questions which any minister of the gospel must surely take seriously. Indeed they are questions which continue to gnaw away at me and within me and with which I have to live. Without in any way minimising the extent of human suffering or its effects, I find that as well as the questions and the anger, I need also to hold within me the resilience, courage, fortitude and determination of those who suffer, as well as the enormous human goodness, generosity and kindness, indeed very often heroism, which is to be found in those who care for the sick and the suffering, whether professionally or because that is the way it has turned out. Here I find something of the self-giving, self-offering, self-forgetting love of God. It does not answer the questions. It does not make them any less relevant, but I have always found that it does help me to see the situation as a whole. If we are to see it as a whole, we recognise the stark reality of suffering humanity, but we recognise it in the context of the response of human love and affection, of generous self-giving. The one does not eradicate the other, nor will it ever. It does, I believe, find its perfect expression in the cross of Christ, in the anguished and tormented death upon Calvary, in those nailed and bleeding hands fastened to the cross, hands which were always so ready to touch and to hold. Even in Jesus' suffering and death, even in the moments of his God-forsakenness, God is intimately present, holding, loving, supporting and sustaining, just as I believe he continues to be in suffering humanity today.

9

Serving

*Jesus rose from supper, laid aside his garments, and girded himself
with a towel. Then he poured water into a basin, and began to wash
the disciples' feet and to wipe them with the towel with which he
was girded.* (John 13:3–4)

One of the many pictures we have of Jesus during Holy Week
is that of his washing the disciples' feet. St John tells us that
after supper together, Jesus rose from the table, put a towel
around his waist, and began to wash the disciples' feet. Not
surprisingly Peter, the lively and impetuous one, protests
loudly. Why on earth is this person, the one they call lord
and master, doing the job of a servant and slave? He could
not make head nor tail of it. Indeed there is a hint of real
frustration and anger in Peter that Jesus should even think
of performing such a demeaning and menial task.

Yet Jesus perseveres quietly – he simply gets on with the
job, responding calmly to Peter, yet washing his feet too! The
social customs and accepted norms of the day are completely
stood on their head. Here was the master and lord, not lording
it over others, not exercising his authority in an authoritarian
way, but, rather, performing an act of humble service, show-
ing himself to be the servant and slave of all.

In this act of foot washing, Jesus underlines what has been
true from the beginning and which must be true to the end,
that his way and the way of those who would be his disciples
is, before it is anything else, a way of service.

For any Christian, service is not an optional extra, not
something we can choose to engage in if we feel like it. It is
an integral part of what we are called by Jesus Christ to be.
It is not a matter of do-gooding or the 'social gospel'; genuine

Christian service arises out of the deep reverence, awe and respect that one person must have for another, made as we all are in the image and likeness of the eternal God.

If we reflect upon this theme of Christian service, a number of possibilities spring readily and naturally to mind. For almost every congregation of every Christian denomination there are activities and services directed towards the more needy members of the local community quite irrespective of religious commitment – schemes for the unemployed, the elderly, the handicapped, the sick, the bereaved, those who are mentally ill and find themselves ill at ease in the local community; there is a caring for and about the vulnerable and those people most at risk. Such work is often done in conjunction with other statutory and voluntary groups. Indeed many of the varied voluntary groups beyond the bounds of the churches comprise large numbers of Christian people who see this involvement as their particular contribution to society at large.

There are too, I would suspect, many anonymous 'servants' who in the course of their daily round consider the whole of their lives to be inspired by the example of Jesus the servant and slave of all – be it housekeeper, school teacher, joiner, bus driver, office worker or unemployed person. I was very forcibly reminded of this recently when visiting one of our church schools in a particularly depressed and needy area of the East End of London. In the basement of the school I noticed there was a washing machine. 'Oh,' said the head-teacher, 'that is where we do the children's washing if the mother is sick or unable properly to look after the child.' It was quite a natural and ready response from the staff – one of the many ways I saw in which they were ready to go beyond the demands of their professional work in real Christian care and concern for others. Such people do not go on endlessly about their faith, they are not necessarily churchy or religious, but they draw much strength, inspiration and courage to persevere from those words of Matthew's Gospel: 'In as much as you have done it to the least of these you have done it to me' (Matthew 25:40).

But it is not just or only a matter of doing. I am reminded of Milton's words, written in his blindness, that they also serve who only stand and wait. It is as much in the being as in the doing that Christian service is effected. In the end it is the readiness to let go of ourselves and to keep our eyes, ears and arms open for our neighbour that is most important.

10

Dying

Then Jesus, crying with a loud voice, said, 'Father, into thy hands I commit my spirit!' And having said this he breathed his last. (Luke 23:46)

Death is not a very popular subject. Indeed in our society it seems that almost every measure is taken to ensure that we do not come face to face with it, despite the fact that once born into this world, the only certain fact ahead of us is that we shall depart from it. Death comes to us all. I can still remember very vividly my grandmother's death when I was a child. The curtains in the front room were closed, as were the front room curtains of close neighbours. She was laid out in the same front room, and relatives and acquaintances came to pay their last respects and fond farewells in the days between her dying and the funeral. My sister and myself were also taken in to see grandma – there was a deep sadness, yet, at the same time, a real peace, and in that whole process a letting go. Our modern society finds it difficult to cope with the process of dying and death. Perhaps the reality of it all is too much to bear – it is something to get out of the way quickly with as little upset and inconvenience as possible.

Good Friday sets before us the stark reality of Christ crucified. All four Gospels have extensive accounts of the last days and hours of Jesus' life, accounts which tend to heighten the drama of the event, yet which straightforwardly and movingly tell the story of the death of this one man, Jesus of Nazareth. Perhaps it is because the story is so familiar that the pain and horror of it seem not quite to touch us in the way they might. It is rather like those scenes on the television screens which night after night make their way into the cosy comfort of our living rooms, right in front of our armchairs – scenes of violence, torture, war, killing, destruction and death; brutal scenes taking place right before our eyes, and yet somehow we feel distanced and detached from the terrible reality so that we are unable to identify with and enter into the tragedy.

It is the same for the death of Jesus. We may see a passion play, watch a dramatic or even 'straight' reading of the passion narrative, attend the solemn celebration in the liturgy and worship of the Church, yet never quite get to the reality of it . . . that is, not until we ourselves are confronted with death right where we are.

From the very beginning, though, Christians have spoken of glorying in the cross of Christ. The cross of Jesus Christ has become *the* Christian symbol, *the* main point of focus whatever our Christian tradition may happen to be. This is a pointer to the fact that the cross, death and dying are, Christians believe, a stage in that altogether larger and greater design of God for us all, of transformation, change and resurrection; 'the life of thy faithful people, Lord, is changed not taken away', is the way one of our funeral prayers puts it.

The process of dying, I would suggest, is not unlike the process of being born, and this is, perhaps, a helpful way of approaching it. Here we are in the 'womb' of this world, the limitations of time and space surrounding us and hemming us in until finally our journey through this world leads us out and beyond and into an altogether new and different future, a future about which there will surely be that same sense of curiosity, excitement and adventure as when we entered this life.

Of course there is bound to be sadness and sorrow for those left behind, and I would in no way wish to minimise that. But for our loved one who has gone before us, there is now true freedom, real fulfilment and the joy of discovering that we are still one in the risen and living Lord, the one who was dead and behold he is alive for evermore.

11

Rising

But the angel said to the women, 'Do not be afraid; for I know that you seek Jesus who was crucified. He is not here; for he has risen, as he said.' (Matthew 28:5–6)

One of the most impressive and moving celebrations of Easter I have ever experienced was not in a Christian country but in the oppressively Stalinist Romania some twenty-five years ago. It was Easter eve, the final day of the forty days of Lent (and in Orthodox countries the fasting is taken very much more seriously than in the West, as is the feasting). It was nearly midnight and a large crowd had gathered around the cathedral, the church being overlooked by the securitati guards mounted on the National Assembly building nearby. It was a hushed and expectant crowd, waiting for the strike of midnight. It was a very dark night, with hardly any street lighting at all, a powerful reminder of the darkness of death and the grave. On the strike of midnight the Patriarch appeared from within the dark and empty church in stunning white and gold vestments holding aloft a blazing torch. Here was a powerful symbol of Christ emerging from the tomb resplendent in resurrection glory. 'Christ is risen', he boldly and confidently announced to the crowd. 'He is risen indeed', was the immediate and spirited response. And at once the whole square was a blaze of light and song, with candles and torches flickering among the two thousand or so people gathered there and the triumphal song of Christ's victory over death being repeatedly chanted – 'Christ is risen from the dead and to those in the grave he has brought new life'. The chanting went on into the early hours of the morning and well into the afternoon of Easter day. Then came the feasting with all those things they had done without – wine, beautifully painted eggs and meat, such as could be got in those days. Everywhere on Easter morning the joy and exaltation of Christ's resurrection echoed and reverberated – in the bread shops, on the buses, in the casual exchanges in the streets; no longer, 'good morning, how are you?', but, 'Christ is risen, he is risen indeed'.

However it is celebrated, wherever it is celebrated, Easter is *the* Christian festival, for it celebrates that once upon a time act of God in raising Jesus from the dead. It was a once upon a time act yet also a once for all time act – God raised Jesus from the dead and it is this Jesus that we proclaim today.

In England I suppose we tend to associate Easter with spring, daffodils, bonnets and chocolate eggs, yet even here there is surely a clear message of new life. Perhaps it is that the word 'Easter' is derived from some more primitive pagan festival time, but, as with Christmas, the Church has baptised it, given it an altogether new and definitive meaning. The new life which is evident to us, the green shoots, the colourful hedgerows, where but a month or two earlier there seemed to be nothing at all, are a very powerful symbol of resurrection. Indeed, St Paul, in his Letter to the Corinthians, makes almost exactly the same point about the sowing of a seed in the earth; the seed is apparently quite lifeless and dead, but in time it produces a flower of splendour and beauty – an appropriate image of death and resurrection. The hymn of Thomas à Kempis expresses it exactly: 'oh how glorious and resplendent fragile body shalt thou be.' It is in and through the resurrection of Jesus that we see a foretaste of our own.

'Never allow anything so to fill you with sadness and despondency that you forget the joy of Jesus who is risen', said Mother Teresa of Calcutta, one in whom the risen life of Jesus shines out naturally and powerfully. The same risen life nourishes many evidences of God at work in his Church and in his world. The triumph of Easter is the fact that neither death nor life, nor angels, nor principalities, nor things present, nor things to come, nor anything else in all creation will be able to separate us from the love of God in Christ Jesus our Lord. 'Christ is risen, he is risen indeed.'

12

Waiting

Then Pilate said to him, 'Do you not hear how many things they testify against you?' But he gave him no answer, not even to a single charge. (Matthew 27:13–14)

Waiting is a very common experience and we all know what it is like. We wait in queues – for the bus, in the shops, at the garage, in the traffic – and we often become very frustrated and annoyed.

Then there is a sort of expectant and almost excited waiting, before a special event, before a party or some particular celebration when it seems as if the day and the time cannot come quickly enough.

There is an uncertain waiting, too. We have agreed to meet up with someone, outside such and such a bank, along such and such a street. We have arrived on time, and there is no one around. Will they come or won't they?

Many people experience waiting in a very negative kind of way, and that is particularly true of many of our younger people, waiting endlessly in the dole queue, with little or no prospect of employment; waiting for a letter to come through the post in response to your fifth or sixth application for a job, only to be told there is nothing doing; more waiting, endless waiting, useless waiting.

This same theme of waiting is very much part of the bible story, not least in the events surrounding Jesus' passion and death. One of the very remarkable things which always strikes me about the Gospel accounts of Jesus' arrest, trial and crucifixion, as I come to read them afresh each year, is the fact that Jesus himself remains so silent. He answers never a word.

He waits patiently and quietly, he hands himself over so that they may do their worst with him.

There is no resentment or hatred about his attitude or about his words. Some may consider that figure, bound and crowned with thorns, to be somewhat pathetic and weak. Weakness indeed there is, and it is not merely human weakness, but divine weakness as well. God, in Jesus Christ, is handing himself over, so to speak, daring, taking the risk that he might be done to death.

But in that silent, weak and fragile figure standing before Pilate – then, later with his arms outstretched on the cross – there is divine strength. All around him is noise, plotting, whispering, and much frenzied activity. In the midst of all that is the silent strength of the one who waits.

This surely must say something to us about our own experiences of waiting. On the whole we tend to treat waiting as time lost, a waste. In the passion and death of Jesus we see this idea being turned upside down. The very point of his weakness in waiting becomes his greatest strength. So perhaps there is a need for us to look again at our own waiting, at our own use of time.

Usually when we wait in queues we become more and more furious. We could, though, turn all that negative and destructive energy into something positive for God. I find there is always someone in a queue who is cheerful and outgoing, and what a difference it makes; someone who simply stands there with a quietness and serenity which brushes off on others. The waiting might offer the few moments when we can snatch a quick prayer – the God-given moment today in that queue, in that waiting, a gift to be savoured and used instead of resented and rejected.

Similarly, perhaps that apparently hopeless and useless kind of waiting can become something more for us, can become a time when we pause and draw much more closely to ourselves all those other people in the world who have to face endless, useless waiting – in refugee camps, in war-torn areas of Africa and the Middle East, those in prison for their faith and for conscience's sake, all waiting endlessly, uselessly.

Perhaps we can use our waiting, then, as a means of entering into their waiting. Our frustration can become a prayer with them and for them that the Lord Jesus Christ who willingly gave himself up to waiting might be with them to sustain them that they might know his presence just as he promised.

MINISTRY

13

Bishop's Charge for Ordinands*

Train yourself in godliness; for while bodily training is of some value, godliness is of value in every way, as it holds promise for the present life and also for the life to come. (1 Timothy 4:7–8)

There are many and varied occasions when the bishop is called upon to preside, officiate, participate or whatever. There are the big occasions, such as my enthronement weekend, but there are also the simpler, more 'hidden' occasions. I can remember one such 'hidden' occasion when it was both my privilege and sorrow to officiate at the funeral of one of the priests in my former diocese of Wakefield.

He had served in the diocese, in a variety of parochial appointments, for some thirty-one years. His was a truly great ministry, remembered with appreciation and thanksgiving by very many people across the diocese, not least by those quite outside the confines of 'church'. He had never sought the limelight, but from the very beginning had that obviously simple and clear delight in God and in people, and when asked where he might see himself working, he responded, 'Wherever God chooses to send me'. He had never been particularly rich; indeed, at the beginning of his ministry, and for the greater part of it, I think you could describe him as 'poor'. I suspect that when, in recognition of so committed and devoted a ministry, I informed him that I was intending to make him an honorary canon of the cathedral church in Wakefield, he would have been somewhat bewildered and bemused about something which simply would never have entered his head.

*St Paul's Cathedral, Sunday 29 September 1991

I mention all this because I believe that there is too much talk these days about career structures, and I suspect, too, there lurks around in all of us that most fatal aspect of clericalism – status. 'Let it not be so among you', warns the Lord who is calling each of you into his ministry, and note that it is his ministry as deacon or priest with which you are entrusted. No ministry in the Church is yours to possess, yours by right, yours to do with as you will or as you please. The ministry in which you have a part and a share, albeit a distinctive part, is that which Our Lord Jesus Christ, the great high priest of our profession, has entrusted to the whole Church. Your ministry, therefore, is rooted in the place, in the congregation and community to which you are licensed by myself as your bishop. Hopefully, it will be a ministry which is exercised in and among those same people, not over and above them, not apart from them, not idiosyncratically individualistic among them. Your ministry is a gift from God, endued with that power from on high, encouraging, exhorting and enabling the Church to be both the sign and the instrument in the world of God's reconciling and redeeming love – his love for humanity, for the whole of creation.

It is a tall order indeed, and you might as well recognise from the outset that it is a well nigh impossible task to fulfil, as those of you who have already been at it for a year will have begun to discover. Yes, of course, you will need your time management and your organisational skills, and a good many other skills besides, not least with regard to yourselves. But most vital and important of all you need to recognise the weakness and the frailty of this earthen vessel which is you and me, and our own constant and continuing need of God's grace. In setting out your priorities then for ministry, whether diaconal, episcopal, priestly or whatever, there must be the primacy of prayer and worship, of adoration and thanksgiving, of reflection and listening – in short, as the psalmist has it, of hearing what the Lord God would say concerning you. We must not allow ourselves to be so caught up in the 'doing' of our ministry that we neglect the 'being'. Sometimes 'being' with and alongside someone will be the only appropriate exercise of ministry towards them. The trouble is that unless we are actually doing something, we often have the feeling that we are not really being very effective. However, I believe that if we had fewer words and less 'doing', then the whole Church might be better able to hear God's Word more clearly and proclaim it more vigorously and prophetically.

I find, myself, that there are those days and those weeks – these days, most days and weeks – when I wake up and think to myself, 'Dear God, how on earth am I going to make it? How shall I get through and survive?' And somehow at the end of it I do seem to find that I have survived. The 'somehow', I believe, is no fluke or mere chance – it is by the grace of God. And this reflection on how it has been gives me the possibility of becoming less panic-stricken and more ready to surrender myself into the Lord's hands, with the prayer, 'not my will but thine be done, O Lord'. Thus I find my own weakness and feebleness, my own frailty, my own hesitations and anxieties, even my own mistakes and failures, become the very stuff whereby God's grace the more abounds – his will is done almost in spite of me and not because of me. This is just one of the paradoxes of ministry which ensure that we do not become as those who simply lord it over others, as those who know all the answers, as those who have God sewn and tied up!

I can well appreciate that those of you just come from theological colleges and courses will be raring to go, to get stuck into the real thing, wondering just how the Church of England has managed to survive without you and your gifts! Do, though, remember that you are a long-distance runner and not a short-spurt sprinter. In other words, from the start of your distinctive ministry, give yourselves the time and the space not only for recreation but also for continuing and sustained biblical study and reading. I can well appreciate that for some of you the thought of yet another biblical commentary or doctrinal treatise will fill you with horror, yet much of your ministry from the start will be in giving out, not least in teaching. There is a great hunger and a great need for some very basic teaching about the Christian faith, about what we believe and why we believe it. Such teaching will be your responsibility, a clear dimension of your ministry as one appointed and authorised to teach, preach and expound God's Word. So you will need to keep your minds attuned, alive and refreshed by a continuing commitment to study and to the art of communicating what you assimilate in a lively and attractive manner. The worst you can possibly do is to make God boring, and yet just how many clergy succeed in doing precisely that! In your public office it is the faith of the Church which you are to guard, teach and preach, not the latest views about the lost ending of Mark or whatever the current theological fad might seem to be. You will, of course, have your own personal faith, your own views and questions, your own searching and struggling, but you will always need to take heed of St Paul's warning about the risk of so preaching to others that you yourself become a castaway.

This brings me to another important consideration in our Church at the present time and for those of us called to serve in the ministry. If you look around you, it will not take you long to conclude what an extraordinary bunch of people we are. How different we are in a whole variety of ways, and this difference is inevitably taken into the exercise of our ministry. We shall also, I suspect, have differing models of the Church itself, differing models of ministry in our minds. And there is always the temptation to want others to conform to the way I see things, to the way I have got it worked out, because that is the way God has it! That which is one of the strengths of the Church of England is also one of its weaknesses – namely unity and diversity existing together and the delicate interplay there must necessarily be between them. Living with difference and not being anxious about it or threatened by it is very much part of our calling in these days. There are certainly some keenly and deeply felt differences among us from the more serious and weighty matters to the more trivial things such as the removal of a couple of pews from the back of a church or the question of who makes the tea on the third Sunday of the month!

Whenever there is divergence and difference, whether it be at the local parish level, at diocesan level, or within the worldwide Church of God, we need always, I believe, to exercise a proper courtesy and respect towards each other, even towards those with whom we feel ourselves disagreeing most fundamentally. We must learn to listen to each other and really to hear each other, to enjoy each other's company, to remain in that koinonia, that communion and charity of the Holy Spirit which is the bond of peace and which alone is able to hold us together one with another, in the one Lord and Saviour Jesus Christ. We need to give each other the space and the respect that each is due as individuals created in the image and likeness of the eternal God.

This business of learning to live with each other, of learning the courtesy and respect that we gladly and generously extend to each other, needs to begin right here and now; we need to work at it and work with it. We must not dismiss each other out of hand or write each other off. After all if the Church is unable to be a real and effective sign of living with difference, what hope is there for any kind of effective communication of the gospel message of reconciliation, healing and redemption. When you begin to shout slogans at each other always remember the words of Sam Goldwyn: 'To every complex question there is always a simple answer – and that answer is always wrong!'

Given the fact that there are differences and divergences, there are also norms, and it is only by being committed more deeply and fully to these norms that the bonds of communion among us can be sustained, even enhanced. I suppose that many of you may well have heard of the existence of the Canons of the Church of England, but have not ventured too much into them. They do in fact make interesting and informative reading, but the Canons are not there to impose a rigid and authoritarian kind of strait-jacket upon us; rather they offer a framework whereby we may all remain together as members one of another in the Church of England. There is a great danger in so many places these days of a narrow parochialism which is no more and no less than a rampant congregationalism. At this point, Canons C26 and C27 of the Manner of Life of Ministers and of the Dress of Ministers are, I think, particularly relevant. The first, Canon C26, is a clear commitment: every bishop, priest and deacon is under obligation to say daily the morning and evening prayer, either privately or openly; and to celebrate, or attend, holy communion on all Sundays and other principal feast-days. We are also to be 'diligent in prayer and intercession', in examination of our conscience and in the study of the holy scriptures and such other studies as pertain to our ministerial duties. The second paragraph of this Canon reminds us that we are not to give ourselves to such occupations, habits, or recreations as do not befit our sacred calling, or may be detrimental to the performance of the duties of our office, or tend to be a just cause of offence to others. So we are reminded both of 'the great excellency' and of 'the great difficulty', as the Prayer Book has it, of the ministerial office to which we are called. As a person publicly authorised and empowered in the Church, there must at all times be both an integrity and a consonance between the public and the private aspects of our life and living. At all times we should be diligent to frame and fashion our life and that of our family according to the doctrine of Christ, and to make ourselves and them, as much as in us lies, wholesome examples and patterns to the flock of Christ.

Canon C27 is about the dress of ministers, which may seem a somewhat superficial, frivolous matter, but which is something other people are quick to note and which says much about the way we ourselves perceive and present our own ministry. The Canon speaks of our mode of dress as being suitable to our office; and, save for purposes of recreation and other justifiable reasons, shall be such as to be a sign and mark of our holy calling and ministry. This does not, of course, mean that we have to sleep in our dog collar or wear our cassock, or other more exotic items, at every occasion. It is about the need to be appropriately dressed in the exercise of our public office and duty and in the conduct of public worship so that we can be readily and easily identifiable as the person we are. It is also about personal presentation and that degree of professionalism which is to be expected in the Church's ministers these days – about punctuality and careful preparation, both practically and spiritually, for the conduct of worship, the reading of scripture, the preaching of sermons and not least those occasional offices which we can so often resent but which continue to offer the opportunity for seeds to be sown, for a word of life to be spoken to those many people who only come into our churches on those 'hatches, matches and despatches' kind of occasions. We must not waste our energies in setting up even more barriers for people to cross; rather let our energies be directed into the more creative and positive ways of meeting individuals where they are, and, after the frame and fashion of the Good Shepherd himself, let us take and lead them into the green pastures of the kingdom.

Clearly there are many other things which could be said. I hope I have been able to draw your minds towards really just two or three main areas which came to me as I reflected on what I might appropriately set before you in my charge to you at this time of your ordination. One final thing I would say is this: I would hope that if by any chance things did begin to go wrong, if substantial difficulties or problems were to arise, either with regard to your ministry, or with regard to yourselves more personally and your family, you would not hesitate to come and share these with your area bishop or myself or one or other of the archdeacons. It is always much better if we know about something at the earliest possible time rather than being left to pick up the pieces when the proverbial horse has bolted. The exercise of authority and discipline is committed to the bishop of the diocese, but it is an authority to heal and not to hurt, to build up and not to destroy. It is a discipline to be ministered with mercy and a mercy to be exercised with firmness. Fundamental, in any case, to all our ministries must be the diaconal aspect at all times and in all things. Before all else the bishop is deacon to those he ordains and for whom he has a pastoral care; the priest is deacon to those among whom he ministers. So we need to ensure that there is a real openness and trust between us; and you need to know that even when you have fallen very far, you may, yes, get a pretty straight response; but it will be in the context of a real concern and deep love for you as a brother or sister in Christ, and for your well-being and wholeness in the Lord.

In these last hours before your ordination let there be a real relaxing and letting go and a real readiness to trust wholly in God's love and God's grace – a casting of all your cares upon the Lord who calls you just as you are here and now, just as he called his first followers beside the Galilean Sea. Present, but unseen, in the sacramental act of the laying on of hands in the course of your ordination is Jesus Christ the great high priest – the servant king. It is he who lays his hands upon you and those hands are scarred. They bear the marks of suffering, passion and death, and are a sign to us and to the whole Church of that one perfect and sufficient sacrifice which he made upon Calvary's tree and into which we are to be drawn ourselves more deeply and mysteriously as we are entrusted with a share in his ministry. Look forward then, yes, with apprehension and perhaps with a certain anxiety; but look forward, too, expectantly and joyfully to that which he is calling you to do and to be, and to that which he will work in you through that power from on high, the gift of the Holy Spirit, in order that you may indeed exercise that ministry entrusted to you in the Church. Remember that whatever you do, in word or in deed, do everything in the name of the Lord Jesus Christ giving thanks to God the Father through him.

14

The Ministry of David Diamond*

Whether we live or whether we die, we are the Lord's. (Romans 14:8)

It is some twenty-three years ago that I remember first coming to this church of St Paul, Deptford, for the inauguration of Father Diamond's ministry in this parish. As with any new beginning there was an air both of excitement and expectancy. He had already begun to make a name for himself because of the extraordinary rapport he had with young people, because of his great love for them and indeed all those committed to his care; he had a deep concern that each and every person should come to know and to love the Lord Jesus Christ, the Lord and Saviour to whom he had given himself and his life, fully, wholly, and completely in the ministerial priesthood. For Father Diamond priesthood was no theological concept, something to be argued about and discussed endlessly; priesthood was a charge from the Lord – 'feed my sheep, feed my lambs'. It was to be lived and to be got on with, and the sheep and the lambs were certainly fed by him and through him. He had a remarkable way of setting people at ease, whoever they happened to be – the high and mighty, the poor and needy, as well as the sinful and the downright wicked. He was not simply a priest, a minister of the Lord's healing and reconciliation; he was, above all, a friend. That is, I suspect, what will be foremost in many of our minds at this moment. We have not simply lost our parish priest, a man of God; but a man of the people, a true friend, a friend of God and a friend of mine.

*The funeral of Father David Diamond, Thursday 10 September 1992

Each of us will, of course, have our own fund of stories to tell about him. I have to say that I personally owe him more than I can say for the way he shaped my own understanding and practice of the ministerial priesthood. St John's Hall, Tuebrook, in the early sixties was a seething mass of young people, not least on a Friday night. It was the time when Liverpool's Cavern was thriving. I can remember one such night very well, when the ever popular Wild, Wild Clubs were to be performing. It was a holy day of obligation, so, of course, no Mass, no dance. We scraped through the Mass, and there were present literally scores of girls and boys who would never in the ordinary course of events have dreamed of entering a church building. Then, on entering the youth club, Father Diamond said, 'Oh farv, we're short of helpers tonight, would you please stand guard at the emergency door?' What he'd omitted to tell me was that a marauding gang from Scotland Road was expected and their accomplices were to let them in through the emergency door. He was always well informed, he knew the buzz. We survived the night – but only just.

To the very end, though, young people, their well-being and welfare, were his real priority. The Isle of Man holidays were part of the annual round in Liverpool and in Deptford, and visits to some main centre would often result, later in the stay, with a visit from the local CID whose searches usually revealed a veritable aladdin's cave of goodies stuffed in shirts and socks in cases under the beds. Father Diamond, though, was always ready to plead the cause of those so apprehended.

All this and much more besides was, though, no mere social gospel; he was not simply a do-gooding clergyman. His whole priestly ministry sprang from that which is central to the catholic tradition in which he had been nurtured at St Peter's, Streatham, namely the fact that God in Christ became incarnate of the Virgin Mary and was made man. God in Christ had become one of us, he had entered in and among us and taken upon himself our wayward and fragile human nature; and nowhere is this more clearly celebrated and proclaimed than in these saving mysteries which this day we offer in thanksgiving for the life, ministry and friendship of David Diamond. For here in the sacramental symbols of bread and

wine is the focus of God's continuing and abiding love for us, for all his people, for his entire creation. Here the process of transformation is both celebrated and effected, as each of us is drawn into the movement of Christ's own self-offering to the Father. Here God's unending and eternal love continues to be profusely and generously given, so that the priest has no alternative other than that his own life and ministry should be modelled in his own generous self-giving love towards others. 'It is the Mass that matters', Father Diamond would often say; and it was the Mass which ever remained for him the point of departure and of return.

The generosity which is in the heart of God was also reflected in the overwhelming generosity of Father Diamond. No matter who you were, you would always be assured of his kindness and his generosity; he would give you his last penny and indeed what he hadn't got and what he couldn't afford as well. There was a profligacy and recklessness about the way he lived his life – always for and on behalf of others, never in the pursuit of his own self-interest or self-aggrandisement. There were those who would sometimes be cynically dismissive of what he was about, as if he fostered a personality cult. Nothing could be further from the truth; what he was about had been modelled already for him in the remarkable priestly lives of the catholic revival. Stanton, Mackonochie and, not least, Jellicoe were his heroes. Of course he was an individual and his style highly individualistic and thank God for that. Would that there were more in the Church today of his hue. He did not care and never thought about what he ought to do next, where he might go or whether he might be preferred. His only concern was the treasure which had been committed to him – the people of Deptford: your well-being and the well-being of your immortal souls. He certainly was no party man. He was not much into committees and groups and so much of that which consumes time and energy in the Church today. Rather for him time and energy were to be spent in the service of his people, in the living of that basic incarnational principle in and among the people he served.

In the end, death came suddenly to him and what a shock it must have been for George, his father, with whom he had just begun a much needed holiday in Scotland. Already he

had been warned by the severe heart attack he suffered at Walsingham, and we know that he wasn't the sort of person who once on his feet would be likely to be careful for or about himself. 'Oh farv, have another gin', he would still say; he would still accept yet more demands on his time and himself when he should actually have taken less; still be in and out of court; away with youngsters; arranging the Deptford Festival – concerned as well for the old folk and their needs and treats. There was no way in which he was going to ease up. But this was the person and the priest that he was and that he fervently believed God had called him to be, and in the end there was no tearing him away from that.

So, today, our hearts are heavy with sadness and sorrow; we have all lost a very good friend. Equally surely there must be great thankfulness and praise to God who created David John Diamond, and gave him to us. Our sympathy is surely with George and with his brother, Christopher. Our two mothers, Father Diamond's and mine, died on the same day – now he will know their greater joy. I am utterly convinced, though, that he would not wish us to spend too much time in grief and sadness, but rather celebrating and living more fully and joyfully the risen life of Our Lord and Saviour Jesus Christ, seeking to be drawn ourselves and to draw others more deeply towards the heart of God's eternal love, into whose safe-keeping we now entrust our priest and friend, David. The Lord gave, the Lord has taken away, blessed be the name of the Lord.

I will conclude in a way which I am sure Father Diamond would himself wholly approve. He greatly appreciated and enjoyed the musical *Oliver*; he had seen it many times and had the tape of some of the more popular songs. His undoubted favourite was 'Consider Yourself At Home', and in a way this sums up very appropriately his entire priestly ministry both in Liverpool and Deptford. After all, how often has he said precisely that to you and to me. Now may he have the reward of hearing his Lord and Saviour saying to him, not only 'well done good and faithful servant', but also more cheerfully – 'consider yourself at home'. So, David, we bid you farewell and we entrust you gladly, willingly and confidently to the God who sent you among us. Go then in the name of God

the omnipotent Father, who created you; go in the name of Jesus Christ Our Lord, Son of the living God, who bled for you; go in the name of the Holy Spirit, who has been poured out upon you. And may blessed Mary, St Paul and all the saints pray for you and also for us; that, as on earth we join the whole company of heaven in their unending song of praise, we may all at length come to share the glory and the joy of Christ who is risen and who has promised us all, 'Lo, I am with you always even to the end of time'.

Whether we live or whether we die we are the Lord's.

15

Renewed for Service*

The Spirit of the Lord God is upon me. (Isaiah 61:1)

I have been dipping again into Owen Chadwick's *Life of Michael Ramsey*, and as I read once more through the various chapters it strikes me what an odd lot the Lord chooses to serve him in his ministry. It really is quite astonishing, as Ramsey's person and personality emerge, that he did actually make it to ordination at all. Looking at the criteria for selection in the current Advisory Board for Ministry Handbook and looking back on the early days of my own movement to ordination, I wonder about that for myself also. With his mobile eyebrows, his lack of manual co-ordination, his intense silences followed by repeated yeses – someone once apparently counted up to twenty or so yeses in succession – he was a most unlikely candidate. He could never make his fountain pen work properly, we are told, and when the ink did not flow the way it should he shook the pen so vigorously that the ink flowed only too well over walls, carpets, fingers and cassocks. On one occasion he celebrated holy communion with the ends of his back braces protruding out of the top of his vestment. Indeed he could be observed wearing the same vestment inside out – so much for the liturgical purists! There was something of the buffoon, the clown about him, the one who was a fool, but a fool for Christ, and a most attractive and winning fool because he was so thoroughly and transparently himself. His thorough-going human-ness was an attractive sign, not only of his greatness, but also of his holiness.

*Eucharist for the Blessing of Oils and Renewal of Ordination Vows, St Paul's Cathedral, Maundy Thursday 1992

It is indeed in and through these fragile, frail and earthen vessels that we exercise the ministry entrusted to us by Christ in his Church, a ministry of so great excellency yet of so great difficulty. John Sanford, in his book *Ministry Burnout*, touches very appropriately on the nature of the ministerial task – the repetitive aspect of much of our work, not least the way we prepare for and conduct the liturgy and worship of the Church; the constant demands made upon us from so wide a variety of people, the impossible expectations of so many; our involvement with education, with homelessness, with drugs, with alcohol and a good deal else besides, as we attempt to ensure the Church, in the place where it is set, responds as best it can practically and effectively in Christian love and service. Then there are the urgent and unexpected things which cut into and cut across the best laid plan, such as the huge bomb explosion a few yards from this cathedral less than a week ago with the clergy being called out as the major incident plan came into action. Such demands, such pressures, such expectations, can lead in all of us to some degree of tension between what I might call the inwardness and the outwardness which arises from the fact of any public ministry. It is something we have to live with all the time, even in the more domestic matter of fact things; for instance, inside you are feeling lousy, ground down, spiritually at a low ebb, not quite up to it, and yet you still have to go into the school to do that assembly, say nice things to the Mothers' Union and woo the choir into singing something more appropriate for the bishop's visit than three anthems in succession. So how do we cope? How do we survive this impossible and crazy business called Christian Ministry, the pattern for which is given us so eloquently in the Lord's washing of the disciples' feet?

I dare to venture that in spite of all we may say, teach or preach, all of us are to a very large extent caught up in 'self-justifying works', so that 'amazing grace' is almost a stranger to us. Yet it is in and through 'amazing grace' that the Lord has laid his hands upon us, to call us out and into a ministry in his Church, and to authorise and empower that ministry entrusted to us. Furthermore it is only in and through amazing grace that our ministry is nurtured, encouraged and enabled, and ourselves built up into a holy temple to the Lord. There is, therefore, an urgent need in our Church for the renewal of all our lives in the power of the Holy Spirit, not least those of us who do exercise a distinctive ministry. We need to reflect deeply and carefully upon what has been laid upon us, so that there shall indeed be a real harmony and consonance between the inwardness and the outwardness of our calling; a harmony and coherence, though, which is only possible to the extent to which we are prepared not to be conformed to the things of this world but rather to allow the transforming power of the Holy Spirit to be at work in every part of us – the dark side just as much as the bright side; in every aspect of our lives so that we may prove what the will of God is, what is good, acceptable and perfect.

Each of us needs to heed the New Testament injunction to watch and pray. We are not to talk about it or discuss it, but actually to get on with it and to do it. Do we make a real priority in our daily pattern for quality time for prayer? Are we able daily to read and reflect upon the Word of God, not simply allowing our eye to scan the page but really giving ourselves the necessary space so that we can inwardly digest the holy scriptures, so that the mind of Christ may be formed in us? For those of us committed more particularly to the sacramental celebrations of the Church's life, is our celebration of the eucharist prepared for inwardly so that it does not become the casual or matter of fact thing that it can so easily be if we are not guarding the Spirit within? Wherever we are in the ecclesiastical spectrum I believe a contemporary writer hits the nail on the head when he warns us that any Christian ministry must be rooted in a permanent, intimate relationship with the Lord Jesus Christ:

> Through the discipline of contemplative prayer, Christian ministers have to learn to listen again and again to the voice of love and to find there the wisdom and the courage to address whatever issue presents itself to them. Dealing with burning issues without being rooted in a deep personal relationship with the Lord easily leads to divisiveness because before we know it our sense of self is caught up in our opinion about a given subject. But when we are securely

rooted in personal intimacy with the Lord, it will be possible to remain flexible without being relativistic, convinced without being rigid, willing to confront without being offensive, gentle and forgiving without being soft, and true witnesses without being manipulative.

Is our life and ministry so conformed to the following of Jesus in the way of the cross that others find it possible to follow too?

The Spirit of the Lord God is upon me.

It is well that we should record, too, the being and end of all our ministries. The Spirit is given, whether to deacon, bishop or priest, in the first place for service. There is a fundamental kenotic aspect to all our ministries. All of us are here to serve the Church, to enable the Church to be truly the place where the good news is announced to the poor, where release of prisoners and recovery of sight for the blind is declared, where the broken victims may go free, the place and the people among whom week by week, day by day, the year of the Lord's favour is proclaimed. We are called to serve this mission, the mission of God in sending his only begotten Son for the salvation of the world, and how desperately our world today needs to hear these tidings of good news; yet still, like the first disciples, we are lured into scrapping and squabbling over status, power and authority, scoring points over each other, making snide remarks, only too ready to seek out the worst, wanting to lord it over others: 'But let it not be so among you, for I am among you', says the Lord, 'as one who serves.' The ministry entrusted to us is surely his service; for what we preach is not ourselves but Jesus Christ as Lord with ourselves as servants for Jesus' sake. As Michael Ramsey, with whom I began, so often reminded us, 'Thank God often and always'. So let our hearts be full of thankfulness that he has called us and that he does use us, warts and all, just as we are. Michael Ramsey continues:

There will come through the years a tendency to take God's goodness for granted. Thank God, carefully and wonderingly, for your continuing privileges and for every experience of his goodness. Thankfulness is a soil in which pride does not easily grow.

A good sense of humour too, I would suggest, is a soil in which pride does not easily grow, provided that we laugh *with* friends and disciples and not *against* them or at their expense. A sense of proportion and a sense of humour are marks of the ministry of him who has called us to be with him in his continuing work of reconciling the world to himself. Yes, we do have to be serious, for how can we be otherwise as we ourselves are part of that groaning and travailing of the whole created order; but we should never be so intense and serious as not to be able to laugh at the absurdities of life, at the foolishness of God's call of us and at our own absurdities. Laughter here on earth is, I believe, an echo of the laughter of heaven, of the fact that even though we are passing through things temporal we have not lost sight of things eternal, indeed that the kingdom of heaven has drawn near.

So then, let us give ourselves wholly to this one thing – that we will, in the strength of his Holy Spirit, continually stir up the gift of God that is within us to make Christ known to all people.

16

Anglican Catholicism: The Way Forward*

I looked, and behold, a great multitude. (Revelation 7:9)

Liturgy has always been at the heart of Anglican Catholicism as it has sought to set before its adherents the reality of that lovely Prayer Book phrase, 'that in passing through things temporal we do not lose sight of things eternal'. It is precisely in celebration of this truth that many churches are constructed – so that everything about them, the design and architecture, the art and music, the space and silence, the prayer and worship, should be directed to enabling people to catch some glimpse of God's glory.

Attention to the nature of worship is as crucial and vital now as ever it was, and whether the tradition is catholic, charismatic, evangelical or just plain Church of England, much more attention needs to be given to what I would call the ethos/environment aspects of worship. We must focus on its accessibility, but without any loss of its awesomeness; we must have an experience of earth, but also, and just as importantly, an experience of heaven too. Furthermore, are we really expectant about our participation in the Church's worship? Are we really expectant that as we hear God's Word, as we receive devoutly the spiritual food of the most precious body and blood of our Lord and Saviour Jesus Christ, our hearts, minds and lives will be changed and transformed? My hope is that Anglican Catholicism will ensure that the marks of our distinctive Anglican inheritance in worship and its contemporary expression will be encouraged, and that such a movement will recall us to worship as a Church rather than

*All Saints, Margaret Street, Sunday 1 November 1992

as a collection of disparate congregations where it is becoming increasingly difficult, not least among the churches boasting their 'catholic' credentials, to recognise the bonds of our belonging. We need to nurture much more that 'mean', as Cranmer puts it in his preface to the Book of Common Prayer, between 'the two extremes of too much stiffness in refusing' and 'of too much easiness in admitting any variation'. We need more of a commonality in structure and content; a commonality which will be further reflected in the possibility for easy and readily recalled resonances between the public worship and liturgy of the Church and an individual's personal prayer and devotion, the one feeding, supporting and strengthening the other.

This is to begin to move into another area of concern, that which was so fundamental to the whole Oxford Movement and with which we continue to wrestle as Anglicans – our understanding of the nature of the Church, of ourselves as part of the one holy catholic and apostolic Church. For Anglicanism has never claimed a faith of its own but, to use some words of Archbishop Laud, 'only that faith which was once (and but once for all) delivered to the saints' – a faith uniquely revealed in the holy scriptures and set forth in the catholic creeds, a faith which the Church is called upon to proclaim afresh in each generation. It is in the delicate interplay between scripture, tradition and reason that the Anglican method of doing theology has been and continues to be pursued, always recognising that scripture is the normative, primary and controlling source of our authority. As H P Liddon, the considerable tractarian scholar, reminds us: 'We cannot separate the bible from the Church which recognised and has preserved it. The divine book and the divine society are the two factors of the one revelation – each checking the other.' So for Anglicans, tradition is to be understood as that which is consonant with and conformable to the holy scriptures. The former Archbishop of Dublin, Henry McAdoo, wrote that 'the function of the Anglican appeal to antiquity is both faith-guarding and identity-affirming', and it is in this context that reason, our own freedom for exploration, questing and questioning, continues to be pursued.

It is in this context that contemporary issues and questions are also to be explored. As much as anything in the debate concerning the ordination of women to the ministerial priesthood and episcopate there lurks to my mind the substantially more important question of authority and decision-making in a divided Church. There remains a formidable theological task to which I believe Anglican Catholicism must be committed, and where it appears to be somewhat lacking at the present time. Furthermore, in place of the considerably negative mind-set of the catholic movement with its siege and ghetto mentality, there needs to be an altogether more positive participation in and contribution to the many issues before our Church, indeed before the Church Universal; there needs to be a greater openness truly to hear and to seek God's will and God's way for his people. As ever such a will and a way will not always be crystal clear. More often than not the way is opaque and obscure, discerned, paradoxically, more in the unknowing than in the knowing. But it is only in the staying with the questions, in the discussing, the listening, the reflecting and the praying – rather than in the shouting down, marginalising and excommunicating – that we shall, as part of the one holy catholic and apostolic Church, be led towards the truth by him who is the Spirit of truth, the lord and the giver of life. The theological enterprise can be hugely frustrating; it can also be immensely exciting for it is nothing less than an engagement with the deep mystery of God, creator and redeemer of all that was and is and ever will be.

I looked, and behold, a great multitude.

But 'church', its being and nature, cannot remain in the realms of purely theological enquiry. We rejoice that we are 'church', part of the one holy catholic and apostolic Church, through time and in eternity. I deliberately say 'we' – it is an inclusive term, not an exclusive one. To my mind Anglican Catholicism has been too much concerned with ordained ministry and not enough concerned with the ministry and mission of the whole Church. Those of us who are ordained have a particular and distinctive ministry which is at heart wholly diaconal in its exercise; we are stewards and servants at the bottom of the pile rather than at the top so that we may encourage and enable the whole Church to be what together we are called to be – lights in the world, salt to the earth. I would like to see a much greater attention being given to a theology of the laity, a theology which is in no way patronising, but which recognises the primacy and priority of who and what together we are. Whether we are priest, deacon, bishop, churchwarden, organist, in the third row or the back row, together we are women and men baptised into Christ Jesus; once we were no people but now we are the people of God. In other words, the enhanced status, if such terms are at all appropriate, ought to go to the laity rather than to the clergy.

A further difficulty which needs to be addressed is the over-preoccupation with the stuffy and constricting world of the Church, with ecclesiastical politicking, committees, synods, more meetings and yet more paper. The Church is actually sent out and sent forth to be both the sign and instrument of that new and living way forged through the death and resurrection of Jesus. The catholic movement has become immersed within the confines of the Church, even of the sanctuary, whereas in truth the eucharist is the very springboard for mission and the proclamation of justice and righteousness for all – the celebration of God's kingdom come on earth as it is in heaven.

Quite rightly, we have been strong on the Incarnation and the Incarnational principle, and that means that it is out in the thick of things, in the cut and thrust of life, in the conflicts and confusions of each day, that the good news needs to be lived. There is a kingdom agenda – the kingdoms of this world becoming the kingdom of the Lord's Christ, and we participate in that process. We need to beware lest we find ourselves in the same situation of which Thomas Hardy tells in *Jude the Obscure*. Jude finds that his children have committed mass suicide and, still trying to take in the horror of it all, he hears two clergymen passing by his window discussing the eastward position. 'Good God,' cries Jude, 'the eastward position and all creation groaning!' One way or another we all have our 'eastward positions' – those things which keep us from a deep attentiveness to and engagement with the world's groaning. The Anglican catholic movement needs urgently to recover a truly 'engaged' spirituality, where holiness is not a matter of being so heavenly minded as to be of no earthly use, but rather of living a life open to full engagement with God's world, undergirded by a prayer which is equally an openness of heart and mind. Prayer of this kind is truly a venture of faith. It is testing, demanding and costly; it is prayer that requires quality time on the part of us all, so that we can penetrate the vain and confused babblings of ourselves and the world around us, and truly hear the Word of God, which both challenges and encourages us forwards and onwards.

That perspective of forwards and onwards is ours today. Our forebears in the catholic movement were zealous for the transformation of the Church and the conversion of England. That task remains and if we are at all to address ourselves to it then we need not only to recover the full meaning of 'catholic' – in the sense of wholeness and inclusiveness, rather than issue driven and exclusive, and quite irrespective of whether we consider ourselves to be of the affirming variety or any other for that matter – but also to realise that we are being called to look beyond ourselves to the vast and increasing numbers of people for whom the Christian message is either of little importance or totally irrelevant. That is the thrust of the eucharist – we are to go forth to love and serve the Lord, to go with confidence and joy in the name of the risen and living Lord Jesus Christ. We are ourselves to live his risen life, surrounded as we are by so great a cloud of witnesses, and ourselves to be the instruments of the Lord's love in bringing others to faith. Yet all the time we must keep alive that vision of the Church which was so dear to those who have gone before us and with whom in the holy mysteries we are united in that love which knows no end – that vision of the Church of Jesus Christ as a divine society, as a wonderful and sacred mystery: truly a home for sinners and a school for saints.

17

The Ordination of Women: The Debate*

Love is always patient and kind; love is never jealous; love is not boastful or conceited, it is never rude and never seeks its own advantage, it does not take offence or store up grievances. (1 Corinthians 13:4–5)

It is with considerable reluctance and real anguish that I offer my contribution to this debate. Whatever happens at the end of today as we come to vote on the proposed legislation towards the ordination of women we know that the question will not be entirely resolved. It is a question which is on the agenda of almost every Church throughout the world at this time and whichever way this Synod votes the issue and debate will not go away.

I am not, nor ever have been, one of those who believe that it is impossible ever for a woman to be ordained. Furthermore, I have sought wherever possible to affirm and encourage the ministry of women both within my previous diocese of Wakefield and in my present diocese of London.

I am totally committed to the full-time ministry of women in the Church but I am not yet convinced that this should necessarily be in the context of the ministerial priesthood and episcopate. So I suppose I am one of those who remains uncertain – still grappling seriously with questions unresolved. I hope, too, that I can say in all honesty that I am very open to the fact that I may well be wrong.

But today's debate is about a certain legislative package; a series of proposals to put into effect the ordination of women to the priesthood. It is here that I am considerably more

*Speech for General Synod Debate, Wednesday 11 November 1992

certain that this legislation has not got it right; in fact I have
strong hesitations and reservations about its aims, tone and
possible effects on the Church of England. As a Synod we
should have the courage to face the fact that we have not got
it right.

I speak as one who from the very moment of having been
entrusted with episcopal ministry some seven years ago has
been personally involved in seeking as constructive a way
forward as possible; also as one who has been closely involved
more widely within the Anglican Communion, as a member
of the Eames Commission – a Commission which as much as
anything sought to ensure a real and continuing space for
those unable to accept women's ordination.

There are two particular points I would like to address.
First of all I want to look at the statement in one of the
documents issuing from the Movement for the Ordination of
Women, that following a vote in favour, this legislation 'makes
provision for everyone to carry on as usual within the
Church'. But, I ask myself, what if the twelve, or however
many they are, diocesan bishops opposed to the legislation
actually did make all the declarations under Section 2 part
2, which they would be perfectly entitled to do, and which
are included as having been given as 'a generous offer from
the majority to the minority', thus making it impossible for
women to minister in their dioceses? Would this be carrying
on as usual when potentially at least twelve dioceses are
closed on the very grounds of ministerial order; not because
of finance or numbers or deployment, but simply and solely
on the grounds of that order which I believe to be of the
very essence of the Church, where the interchangeability of
ordained ministers is a potent sign of communion, of what it
actually means to be a church?

And if we really are not expecting that the provisions of
this particular clause are going to be used, then why are they
there at all? I believe and have consistently argued that
Clause 2 in Part 2 should not stand as part of this legislation.
If the legislation is passed, my view is that life would become
quite intolerable and indeed impossible for any bishop who
made all the declarations.

It looks like generosity. In fact it is no such thing. But

without doubt its usage, even to a more limited extent, would certainly affect the life of the Church of England – as indeed would the provisions for parishes in Clause 3 of Part 2. Again, what of some of the provisions in the draft 'code of practice'? Note that it is only 'draft' at this stage so there must be some question still as to whether it will remain as it is, or yet be changed out of all recognition.

What about arrangements for ordination? What about arrangements for diocesan, archdeaconry and deanery services, and the circumstances in which 'it would be inappropriate for a woman priest to exercise priestly functions'. Would the situation envisaged by this code of practice enable everyone to carry on as usual within the Church?

I think this is wishful thinking and bears no relation to what would be the real truth of the matter – that this legislation sets before us the actual possibility that the Church of England would in no way 'be able to carry on as usual'.

The second point, and one which gives me the greatest concern, is the position of those who are opposed, for whatever reason, if the legislation goes forward. It is argued that the provisions of Part 2 are offered generously for the well-being and inclusion of those so opposed. I am not personally convinced! The Revision Committee report, GS 830Y, indicates the clear understanding of those who are promoting this legislation. This Synod should be in no doubt about it. Indeed I would not be expecting anything other from those who are so firmly convinced that they are right. The Report concludes that 'the necessary majority in favour today would indicate that a common mind on this issue had in fact been achieved within the Church of England' – a statement I would certainly question and challenge.

The figures from the deaneries throughout England simply do not indicate a real and substantial consensus on this matter. The Revision Committee report further states that when the legislation comes into force it would express the mind of the Church of England on the issue of women priests, 'that women priests *must* be accepted with theological and ecclesiological integrity, and that their acceptance *must* become the new theological understanding of the Church of England' – also that the 'safeguards', as Part 2 is described, are intended 'in order to give opponents an opportunity to plan their future'. Well, that does not sound very much like well-being and inclusion to me.

Indeed, such a view was further underscored by a member of the same Committee presenting the legislation in the debate in November 1989 when it was said, 'we must never lose sight of the basic fact that the various safeguards, i.e. Part 2, are "unusual and exceptional" – exceptional provisions in Clauses 2, 3 and 4 given by the majority to the minority with very strong views'. And why? Well, the reason is very plain indeed – 'so that the minority may have space to assess the reality of the ordination of women as it takes place in our two provinces. However, because these provisions are exceptional they must in the end be seen as temporary'.

Those who are opposed are being given considerable reassurances that all will be well, that the Church of England will continue as ever it has, and that there is a full and equal place for all, particularly those who are unable to accept the ordination of women as priests.

I submit that the reality would be very different indeed and if this legislation is passed the Church of England will without doubt be very different, and those unable to accept this new theological understanding, and are unable to accept it with theological and ecclesiological integrity, will inevitably and increasingly find themselves ignored and marginalised.

Having said this, I shall try to respect with as good and generous a grace as I can whatever decision is reached at the end of this day, praying that God will indeed give me the necessary grace and wisdom to continue in communion and fellowship with all in my diocese whatever their views, and I hope and pray they with me also.

18

The Ordination of Women: Quo Vadis?

And Abraham went out, not knowing where he was to go. (Hebrews 11:8)

In this specially written chapter, Bishop David gives his response to the November vote.

Since I became Bishop of Wakefield in 1985 the issue of the ordination of women to the ministerial priesthood has been a major item on the Church of England's agenda. Already in 1985 the process of the preparation of legislation was underway, and almost immediately I found myself as a member of a group appointed to prepare a Green Paper (GS 738) setting out the scope of the legislation and which would be the general basis, following further debate in Synod, upon which eventually decisions would need to be made for the framing of the actual legislation. The group itself made no recommendations: it merely set out the options, together with the major advantages and disadvantages attaching to them, not least with regard to what was described as 'safeguards' for those unable to accept the ordination of women.

Other groups soon followed in order to take further the legislative proposals, as well as to undertake some much more extensive consideration of the theological arguments for and against the proposal that women should be ordained. It cannot be said that throughout this process I had in any way sought actively to work against the proposals. Indeed, since having become bishop I was more conscious than ever of the need, whilst holding my own views on the subject, to ensure that both sides had the freedom and the space for setting out their views with understanding and with clarity. I had always felt that the matter of women's ordination had the status of a 'disputed question' theologically, a question that was now on the agenda of the mainstream Churches, Roman Catholic and Orthodox (from where indeed some of the most interesting and original recent theological writing has come). My own more specific views about the legislative proposals which will now give effect to the ordination of women in the Church of England are set out in my speech in the General Synod during the course of the debate on 11 November 1992. The text of the speech is set out in the previous chapter.

Towards the conclusion of my speech, I indicated that I would try and respect 'with as good and generous a grace as I can' whatever decision would be made, 'praying that God would indeed give me the necessary grace and wisdom to continue in communion and fellowship with all in my diocese'. These were not empty words. I had pondered very carefully indeed on what I should say in the speech as a whole and not least the conclusion of it. I felt I needed to be as honest and as direct as I could about my personal reaction to the legislation. At the same time I was very conscious of large numbers of people, laity and clergy, in the diocese who took an opposing view and to whom also I had a pastoral episcopal care and responsibility.

For a number of months I had felt that whichever way the vote was to go, bearing in mind the need for the two-thirds majority, the eventual majority over and above that requirement would be very slim on either side. The balance lay in the House of Laity, and this had become very much clearer since the meeting of the separate houses in York in July 1992. I received many requests for press interviews. In the end I decided, on the advice of my Diocesan Communications Officer, that I would give an informal and off the record briefing to the press at London House some three weeks before the debate, but that I should then not say anything further publicly before the vote. Already I felt there had been far too much talking and arguing. Towards the end of that briefing, someone asked the question as to which way I thought the vote would go. I responded by saying that I had a sneaking feeling that 'it would just trickle through'.

So where do we go from here? What does the future hold

for someone like myself, a bishop in the Church of England where shortly it will be canonically possible for women to be ordained to the priesthood? My advice has been sought by numerous people, lay and ordained; and I have attempted to be consistent in what I have put to them. I have been struggling with some of the same basic issues for myself. There is no one clear way forward; rather there are, I believe, a number of options, and the options fall broadly between a desire, readiness and willingness to remain as part of the Church of England which now ordains women; or alternatively, if that is not possible, to leave, taking advantage of the provisions of the financial measure. It could be a costly business if all the clergy who are seriously considering leaving the Church of England, some to take up former jobs, some to seek a ministry in another Church, some prepared to go on the dole, if all these do eventually act upon their current thinking.

For myself I have never made any secret of the fact that my first priority is to remain faithful and loyal to the Church in which I was baptised, in which I have been nurtured, and to which I have happily given twenty-eight years of ministerial service. Why should I leave? Or indeed be expected to leave? At the same time I have no illusions about the fact that remaining as a diocesan bishop opposed to the ordination of women will face me with considerable anomalies.

The legislation itself is not a one-clause measure. It comprises three parts, the second of which, bearing in mind the fact that there continues to be considerable opposition to the ordination of women, enables the bishop of a diocese in office at the relevant date, i.e. the promulgation of the Canon, to make one or more of three declarations: (a) that a woman is not to be ordained within the diocese; (b) that a woman is not to be instituted or licensed to the office of incumbent or priest-in-charge of a benefice or of a team vicar for a benefice within the diocese; (c) that a woman is not to be given a licence or permission to officiate as a priest within the diocese. If all three parts of the declaration are made by a diocesan bishop, then the diocese would become what has been described as a 'no go' area, except that such a declaration would not prevent a woman officiating as a priest in a church or chapel for one period of not more than seven days in any period of three months without reference to the bishop or other ordinary. So the question is whether the Bishop of London will as diocesan bishop make one or more of the declarations, being mindful of the fact that any such declaration or declarations would actually bind all other bishops in the diocese. However, since the diocese comprises what is actually a unique area system within the Church of England, the diocesan, under the formal scheme signed on 19 July 1979, delegated to the area bishops complete episcopal and pastoral authority within their area, subject only to very minor exceptions. Thus the area bishops are all but diocesan in name. They themselves are unable to make the declarations, but to all practical intents and purposes they could act in precisely the same way as if the declarations had been made by them even if I as diocesan eventually decide not to make the declarations. To make declarations would certainly be consistent with my own individual position with regard to the legislation, and this is one clear option which is open to me. I am under no illusions about the disappointment, frustration and anger that this would cause the constituency which supports women's ordination. Not to make the declarations would cause similar feelings and expressions in the opposite constituency. Ought the legislation to have presented any individual with so impossible a decision? Already in my speech during the debate I expressed my own feelings that this particular clause is unworkable and ought not to have had any place in the legislation.

If a bishop, such as myself, opposed to the ordination of women, were not to make the declarations, the consequence would be that women priests would be allowed to function in the diocese (though then the views and actions of the area bishops would become very relevant). This prompts the further question that if women are allowed to function within the diocese then who would ordain them, licence them etc? Undoubtedly, the very suggestion of a bishop himself opposed to women's ordination allowing the possibility in his diocese raises large and complex questions and inevitably introduces an element of considerable 'anomaly' into the way he then operates as bishop of the whole diocese. If I were to decide not to ordain women myself, but allow the provision for them to minister in the diocese, then part of the bishop's function would need to be delegated to another bishop, either from within the diocese or elsewhere. And if a bishop from another diocese were to be invited in, then an element at least of 'shared' episcopal ministry is introduced, if not 'alternative' episcopal ministry. The diocesan bishop opposed would then be 'recognising' the fact that he continued to exercise the work and office of a bishop in a Church which canonically had made provision for the ordination of women, whilst himself being agnostic about women's priestly ministry.

The mention of 'alternative episcopal oversight' recalls the memory of the four-day long meeting of the House of Bishops in Manchester in January in order to address precisely this matter. Guarantees had been given that those opposed 'would have no less place in our Church', and that 'careful provision' should be made to respect as far as possible this position. However, until January there was no real telling what this 'careful provision' might be. The atmosphere of the bishops' meeting in Manchester was tense, and, as the diplomats say, there was a full and frank exchange of views. Quite rightly the House had to address how it should take forward the arrangements for those women for whom the Synod vote had opened the way towards ordination, and we spent time carefully discussing what arrangements would need to be in place so that vocations to the priesthood could be tested. A paper from the Chairman of the Advisory Board for Ministry was tabled and discussed, the broad basis of which formed part of the statement from Manchester.

Much more time, however, was given to a consideration about whether provision should be made at episcopal level for those opposed to women's ordination, and, if so, what shape such provision might take. The word 'alternative' was unacceptable. Instead, the bishops' statement speaks of 'enlarged', 'extended' oversight. There was no question of an alternative or separate jurisdiction. The jurisdiction of the diocesan bishop is a clear basic principle of the arrangements which were set out in the statement. Nevertheless, it was admitted that there would be clergy and parishes which expected and needed some additional provision (extended/enlarged) and it was agreed that the regional meetings of bishops should be encouraged to discuss what appropriate arrangements might be made. An altogether new concept was introduced in the shape of 'provincial visitors' – bishops, one in the northern province and two in the southern province, who would be appointed by the archbishops and who would be responsible to them in the collegiality in the House of Bishops to work with the diocesan bishop in enabling extended pastoral care and sacramental ministry to be provided as might be appropriate. They would also act as spokesmen and advisers for those who remained opposed to the ordination of women to the priesthood and would assist the archbishops in monitoring the arrangements made for them.

Such are the broad arrangements which emerged from Manchester and which are to be further discussed when the bishops meet residentially in June. Already, they have been described as unsatisfactory in a number of ways, not least because of their theological untidiness. There is no doubt in my own mind that there are clear anomalies here. Without using them to justify any such arrangements, they are nevertheless the reality of attempting to live with a situation where one ecclesial group, which through its synodical procedures has agreed to women's ordination, allows the continuing and living presence of those who are opposed at every level of its life.

There is no doubt that 'anomaly' has characterised the life of the Church in past eras. Disputes have constantly provoked divided groups and divided bishops. And I suspect that this is almost inevitable in the life of our own Church and communion during what is called this period of reception of women's ministry. It is difficult to attempt theologically to give coherence to the methods and ways of living with this situation. And it was precisely this 'living' within such a situation in the Anglican Communion as a whole that prompted the then Archbishop of Canterbury, Robert Runcie, to set up his commission on communion and women in the episcopate (The Eames Commission as it came to be known) in order to see how it might be possible for those of very differing views to be able to live together 'maintaining the highest possible degree of communion'.

It has been said that the spotlight is on London, and the

decisions that are made here are obviously vitally important for all. Of that I am deeply conscious. I have tried to spell out more fully the nature of the options which are before those whose desire it is to remain within the Church of England, a Church in which very shortly the Canon giving effect to the ordination of women will be promulged. Decisions will have to be made and I have set out above the groundwork for these decisions. The situation could arise whereby a bishop finds that the situation is so impossible that he can no longer remain as bishop and therefore seeks an appropriate appointment elsewhere, say as an incumbent in a sympathetic parish, or indeed, he may eventually feel that he must seek a spiritual home outside the Church of England.

I have stated my own clear option for remaining 'in' and attempting to chart a way forward which is consonant with the provisions of the legislation. The ensuing weeks and months will not be easy, yet even when it is not possible to see the way ahead clearly, faith demands a deeper faithfulness to God and the gospel, and not least to each other. This is a way of recognising that fellowship and communion which is wholly of God's amazing grace, which all of us share by nature of our common baptism into the one Lord and Saviour Jesus Christ.

CHURCH AND MISSION

19

The Reality of the Cross*

God forbid that I should glory save in the cross of Our Lord Jesus Christ, by whom the world is crucified unto me and I unto the world. (Galatians 6:14)

Recently I took the risky and daring decision to clamber up as far as I could get to the top of St Paul's Cathedral. As usual, it was curiosity which rather got the better of me! I had imagined the climbing would stop once I was at the top of the dome, but, no, there were yet more steps until finally I found myself at the foot of the cross, the gold cross which stands in its simple dignity at the top of this great cathedral as a witness. It is a witness to what is central to our Christian faith and Christian life, a witness to the death and resurrection of Jesus. Looking out from the foot of the cross I had a stunning, unique vision of the diocese of London and well beyond – a vision I shall not readily or easily forget. It made me realise that I shall need to see London with Christ from the cross – not as a secular vision of power and domination, but in the power of Christ's transcendent suffering love. That, in the paradox of the cross, means, quite literally, climbing down, for reality is rarely faced three hundred and sixty-six feet above the ground. Reality is faced with your feet firmly on the ground, at the level of the personal, the parochial and the mundane. I am reminded of some words of that great Anglican guide to the spiritual life – Evelyn Underhill. She writes: 'In the depth of reality revealed by the cross, Christianity stands alone.' When I reflect further on that phrase I

*The Enthronement, St Paul's Cathedral, Saturday 14 September 1991

realise just how appropriate it is today, for we are here to face, in the reality of the world, the reality of ourselves.

During my first days and weeks in the diocese I have been trying to get at least my ear to the ground. I have spent a good deal of time listening, and I intend to go on listening. I have listened to a good deal of advice of the 'if I were Bishop of London' variety. I have listened to quite a number of individuals and groups both clergy and lay, women and men, because I believe profoundly that listening and making time for people must be a priority in any episcopal ministry. Moreover, listening is a real and effective sign of that deep bond of communion and fellowship which is given us in Christ. I have heard about the concerns of the parishes and the areas, I have heard about social responsibility and education, about clergy and lay training; I have heard about buildings and brass (that's a northern word for money), and very many other matters which leave me in no doubt whatever that the realities of the diocese can only be faced from the cross – the reality of the Church, the reality of the world, the reality of ourselves.

First then, the reality of the Church. The diocese has been variously described, by some negatively, I regret to say, as for example – 'a poisoned chalice', 'a can of worms', 'a bed of nails', 'a cross'. So where do we begin? I use the 'we' not to sound officially or pompously episcopal, but because what is being done here today, whilst it is focused in myself as bishop, is not just or only to do with me. It is about us, all of us beneath the cross and within the cross, as we set out together to fulfil the commission given us of telling out and telling forth the good news of the death and resurrection of Jesus.

But is there any good news worth telling? As I have listened, the reality has become very clear to me that in spite of the difficulties and divisions, the struggles and problems, there is still good news. There is the good news of much faith and faithfulness among clergy and laity alike. People are simply getting on with the ordinary business of the Church's ministry and mission, enabling communities to worship, pray and meet together – where rich and poor, employed and unemployed, heterosexual and homosexual, families and

single parents, young and old, find themselves in the same
place, at the foot of the cross; where those at the margins,
those who feel themselves alienated and outcast, are affirmed
and accorded that dignity which is the right of each person
created in the image and likeness of the living God. There is
the dedication and commitment of very many Christian
people, ordained and lay, not just for the well-being of the
Church, but so that the Church might reach out more effectively in love, compassion and service in the world, so it can
extend that fullness of life which Christ wills for all. There is
the contribution of countless lay Christians in a wide variety
of voluntary, charitable and community concerns. There are
a large number of Christian people, too, striving to live out
the integrity of their faith in the complex world of today,
where difficult and hard moral and ethical decisions are to
be made in commerce and industry – in the light of the cross.
And, of course, in all of this we rejoice that we share the
privilege of Christian ministry and mission with our sisters
and brothers in Christ of other Churches. Our common and
complementary ministry is rooted in our common baptism
into the one Lord and Saviour Jesus Christ – 'Know ye not
that so many as were baptised into Christ Jesus were baptised
into his death'. I pledge myself to do all I can in this diocese
to further, deepen, enliven and enrich our personal relationships and Christian mission.

God forbid that I should glory save in the cross of Our
Lord Jesus Christ, by whom the world is crucified to me
and I unto the world.

There is also, and inescapably, the reality of the world, of
London, of this capital city and of the diocese which comprises
some eighteen boroughs. It is a large and complex area with
many problems yet huge possibilities. Any newcomer to the
capital, or someone like myself coming back after a number
of years, cannot help being impressed by its liveliness and
vibrancy, by the rich variety and diversity of its people, by
its unique cultural heritage – still, I believe, the best in the
world. But then, as I experience it as it is, with the pushing
and shoving, the traffic jams and exhaust fumes, the litter
and dirt, I begin to wonder where our London pride has gone.

What has happened to that sense of personal responsibility for how things are and how they ought to be? I wander but a few yards from my own home in Westminster only to discover people sleeping in doorways and under arches; and these are but a handful of, for example, three hundred or so each night who file through the crypt of St Botolph's Church hardly a stone's throw from St Paul's. Why is it that a Roman Catholic parish in Acton finds itself serving two hundred and fifty meals a day to homeless people? Not to mention the long and impressive tradition in this area of the Salvation Army. I rejoice that the Christian Church is making such a major contribution, yet the scandal of the cross confronts and challenges us all further to resolve this massive presence of some thirty-two thousand households accepted as homeless by the London boroughs. What we have here is not just or only a matter for 'them' – the government, the local council or whoever. Too often we excuse any positive action on our part by shifting the responsibility on to someone else. What is it within ourselves, within our society as a whole which has given rise to so huge a problem, concentrated as it is on the streets of this great city?

I have already mentioned Evelyn Underhill. She was a Londoner. She lived, as many Bishops of Kensington have lived, in Campden Hill Square. But her spiritual director, the great Baron von Hügel, did not allow her to be concerned only with that part of Kensington. He told her to get out and know the realities of Notting Hill. And so she did. She found the poverty, the hunger and the appalling housing there heartbreaking. She visited and served people in their need. As a result her prayer and worship, her understanding of the eucharist, her knowledge of what it means to be members one of another, was transformed – as was her spiritual discipline and her understanding of the mystery of sacrifice. And it is perhaps in the phrase, 'the mystery of sacrifice', that the real clue to our human and social well-being truly lies. For the cross – the central reality which brought the new community of the Church into being – reminds us that there can be no community without self-giving, generosity and a real commitment to serve one another, in short no community without self-sacrifice. The cross confronts and challenges the possessiveness and acquisitiveness which is all too pervasive in our society today. The mystery of sacrifice does indeed begin with self – with me and with you, with 'us' today. So there are questions posed to us about the capital's role not only in leadership but also in service.

Then there is the reality of ourselves – of who and what we are; and the way in which we are all too ready, in a negative way, to consign individuals into this or that category, to stereotype the ineffable mystery of the presence of Christ in one another. Each of us is a complex creation where shape, size and sexuality, intellect, emotion and feelings, words, actions and so much else besides, constitute that person each of us presently is. We are individuals in company with other individuals in the process of becoming in Christ the persons he wills us and wants us to be. The women at the cross and those who saw the risen Lord were left in no doubt that he treated them in the full reality of who they were. So, too, all of us must treat each other, women and men, lay and ordained, in the full reality of who we are – Christ in us the hope of glory.

And when we come to consider ourselves as a community of people comprising the Church the reality is that we become divided, polarised, alienated from each other. That, St Paul would argue, typifies people left to themselves and their own desires: 'But ye have not so learned from Christ.' One of the results of my own listening has been to conclude that all of us need to work much harder ourselves at listening to each other, at giving each other space. Yes, by all means, we must recognise and face the reality of diversity and of difference, even of division caused by a range of issues in the Church and in the world, not least the debate concerning the ordination of women. We all need to recognise that however things may turn out, there will be a deep pain for all. Meanwhile, as the debate continues in this as in other matters, we need to extend a greater courtesy and a more generous self-giving towards each other, especially towards those with whom we disagree. And where there are such deep, passionate and powerful divergences, everyone needs to work harder in maintaining the bonds of communion between us; rejoicing in the distinctive yet complementary ministries which have been entrusted to women and men within our Church. All of us are called to face the reality of our difference from where we are today, from beneath the cross and within the cross – 'forbearing one another in love, eager to maintain the unity of the Spirit in the bond of peace' (Ephesians 4:2–3).

I have spoken of the depth of reality revealed by the cross. I have endeavoured to be down-to-earth and practical about it; I have done that with one object only in mind – that together we may be renewed in vision and in hope. The cross of gold above St Paul's is a sign to us of that glorious hope of our calling in which already we share here and now – 'for now we are the sons of God and it does not yet appear what we shall be' (1 John 3:2). My vision and my prayer is that the diocese of London shall be a company of Christian people renewed in faith, hope and love, renewed in vision and in glad and generous commitment to facing through the cross the reality of the diocese, the reality of the Church, the reality of the world and the reality of ourselves. We are a diocese with a cross at its centre – a cross of suffering and of death; but through that suffering and death, a cross of gold and glory. So then in all that is before us let us take heart and, as the Epistle to the Hebrews exhorts us, 'let us run with patience the race that is set before us looking to Jesus the author and finisher of our faith who for the joy that was set before him despised the shame, endured the cross and is now set down at the right hand of the throne of God' (Hebrews 12:1–2).

To the same God be all praise, might, majesty, dominion and power now and to the end of the ages. Amen.

20

Where there is Darkness, Light*

This is the day which the Lord has made, let us rejoice and be glad in it. (Psalm 118:24)

There is one school visit among very many that I have made which still sticks in my mind. It was not a church school, but I had been asked by one of those headteachers that even a bishop dare not refuse, to take my bishop's things and show and explain them to the assembled children. The children were invited to enter into this exercise by making suggestions themselves about various of the items. At last we came to the mitre, and as I held it up, one little lad at the back of the hall blurted out: 'He's brought his party hat!' When you come to think about it, that lad could not have spoken a truer word, for this is the day which the Lord has made, let us rejoice and be glad in it.

It is wholly appropriate that the inauguration of my episcopal ministry should begin with a celebration of the eucharist on this day, the first day of the week, the day when from the very beginning Christian people have come together to give thanks for that mighty act of God in raising Our Lord Jesus Christ from the dead. So I make no apology for the fact that I am going to focus on what I believe to be three basic Rs for any Christian – rejoicing, reconciliation and renewal; all of them aspects of the Lord's resurrection.

The first R is for rejoicing. Very often as bishop I find myself placed in the centre of the church, looking out upon a sea of faces, and I begin to think, 'well, God, I am not quite sure what you are making of all this, but really most of them

*Eucharistic Celebration, St Paul's Cathedral, Sunday 15 September 1991

do not look particularly pleased to be here'. The one feature
which runs through the accounts of the appearances of the
risen Lord is the sheer joy of being with him and in the
company of those who share the same joy. There is an infec-
tious enthusiasm and expectation, the sort of enthusiasm and
expectation which I experienced, for example, on my recent
visit to Romania in the midst of much confusion and uncertainty; I discerned it last year even in the abject poverty of
some of the villages of Madagascar. This joy of which I speak
is not the sort of toothpaste smile which pretends that all is
well when manifestly it is not. In some words of Archbishop
Michael Ramsey: 'It is the joy experienced by those who,
come what may, are beginning to know God, to enjoy God in
his beauty and loveliness, and to be exposed to his energies.' It
is the joy of knowing that in spite of all the struggling, the
ambiguity and the uncertainty in which we are presently
caught up, the victory has already been won. Christ is risen.
Jesus is Lord. This is the faith of the Church which is renewed
in us as we celebrate and proclaim in word and sacrament
the death and resurrection of Jesus, and which gives us the
courage and the confidence to face the future, and to move
forward into this future with courage, zeal, and joy. A bit
more joy about our faith would not come amiss!

This is the day which the Lord has made, let us rejoice
and be glad in it.

One of the reasons for our confident and joyful thanksgiving
is that in the resurrection and exaltation of the Saviour our
reconciliation and redemption are accomplished. The first
fruits of the age to come are already at hand; the eucharist
is a foretaste of the banquet of the kingdom. But our reconciliation has been bought through the bloodshedding of Calvary.
It is a celebration of life through death, a transformation from
tragedy to triumph. And it is into this pattern of dying with
Christ in order that we may share his risen life that each of
us has been baptised. We are a reconciled community – with
God and with each other – but are we? Do we allow the
Lord's transforming, redemptive, reconciling love so to suffuse
our hearts and lives that we are, indeed, reconciled? One of
the dictionary definitions of 'reconcile' is 'to restore to friend-

ship or union'. And it seems to me that this is a task to which all of us need urgently to address ourselves. We must become in our day to day lives what we are in the holy communion – very members incorporate in the mystical body, a blessed company of faithful people, a holy fellowship. Of course, there are differences, divergences and disagreements among us across a range of issues, but these should not be the occasions for party strife but rather for an even greater determination not only to maintain but even to build up the bonds of communion celebrated sacramentally in the holy mysteries. Let us seek to rejoice in the rich diversity which God gives us rather than apparently to write off all those who don't happen to see things the way I see them. We need to keep the lines open, the lines of friendship and hospitality, of fellowship and exchange, of prayer and worship and sacramental life together, especially and particularly with those with whom we disagree. Only so shall we be preserved from declining into a cosy congregationalism, a suffocating parochialism, a ghettoism which has never been an aspect of a proper understanding of the one holy catholic and apostolic Church of which we claim to be a part.

This is the day which the Lord has made, let us rejoice and be glad in it.

I come now to the third R – renewal. Renewal is about transformation, new beginnings, it is about expectation and hope for the future. Having spent some weeks listening to a wide variety of individuals and groups expressing their views of the 'now if I were Bishop of London' variety, I realise that the expectations about the new Bishop of London are in fact impossible. Like anyone else I have to begin from where I am, and so I have been having to think carefully about the priorities which I set for myself for the next twelve months. One of these is to ensure that I visit every deanery in the diocese. Another is to ensure accessibility and availability and space for people, not least for the clergy. Further, it is very clear to me that we need a diocesan-wide strategy for mission – an imaginative and forward looking strategy which whilst facing in a severely realistic way the limitations of resources and finance, nevertheless affirms the immense riches already in the diocese as a whole in terms of people and places, and seeks to use these in an enterprising and exciting way for the mission of the Church in the diocese of London into the next century. For in spite of the bad news, there is in fact much good news. And it is up to us to make the good news known, to gain a greater self-confidence about ourselves and that upon which we are engaged – which is no less than God's mission to his world. Let us not forget that we do this with and alongside our ecumenical partners. There is so much more which we can accomplish together and, furthermore, they will often save us from becoming too serious, complacent or even despairing about ourselves. So we need a renewed commitment to the ecumenical enterprise at local level for only so will our unity in the one Lord become a reality in the whole Church of God. Again, there is much to encourage us, but we need to build on that, always consolidating and deepening the experience of our common faith and life in Christ.

But then there is no renewal on the cheap, just as there is no rejoicing and no reconciliation on the cheap. The Christian believer is called to a life of conversion. We may be able to give testimony to a day and a time, but conversion as well as being an event is also a process. We are all called to holiness of life, to work collaboratively and co-operatively together, ordained and lay, women and men, to grow into that full stature of who and what we are, the unique, distinctive and different persons God has made and whom he now enlists in establishing his kingdom of justice, peace and love in the world. So there are priorities to be established for all of us and none more urgent than a deep spiritual renewal – that change of heart and mind, whereby the way we are with each other and among each other is transformed as we proclaim Jesus Christ – he who was dead but is alive forever more, the same yesterday today and forever. All this is not for our own sake, not even for the sake of the Church, but for the sake of the world. For the whole point of our being here at all is that we are sent, sent out to love and serve the Lord in the world; 'where there is despair to bring hope; where there is sadness, joy; where there is darkness, light'. Not being conformed to the ways of this world, but rather being transformed by the renewing of our minds, standing the values of this world on their head, 'for it is in giving that we receive', concludes the prayer of St Francis of Assisi, 'it is in dying that we are born to eternal life'.

Rejoicing, reconciliation, renewal. May these three Rs be our inspiration and guide as together we go forward with a greater sense of purpose, confident that he who has been with us and is with us will also continue with us to the end. 'Fear not', he says, 'I was dead but behold I am alive forever more – I am with you always even to the close of the age.'

21

Agenda for Action*

I came that they may have life, and have it abundantly. (John 10:10)

In his Presidential Address to the London Diocesan Synod in October 1991, Bishop David stressed the need for 'an imaginative and positive strategy for mission within the diocese as a whole'. At the Synod of June 1992, he outlined the priorities of his mission document, 'Agenda for Action', emphasising the importance of a parochial system which can effectively respond to the needs of today's Church and wider community. We print here the edited text of his June Synod address.

Our task in this generation, no less than in the past, is the proclamation of the gospel in worship, word, sacrament and service. In this context I have identified three broad priorities.

1. Worship and Prayer. Worship lies at the very heart of our response to God and is our springboard for mission. Undergirding public worship and prayer is the commitment of every Christian to a personal discipline of prayer and spiritual growth. We are in no state to reach out to others if we ourselves are not growing more deeply and richly in our love of God and of each other. What I am looking for is a Church, a community of believers, vibrant, lively and renewed for mission in the power of the Holy Spirit – a Church more faithful in love and service towards him who is the way, the truth and the life. I have begun to set out something of the

*Diocesan Synod, Monday 8 June 1992

agenda, some of the questions, some of the issues which need to be considered in this regard.

2. Teaching and Nurture. No longer can we assume that people have a rudimentary and basic knowledge of the Christian faith. There is an urgent need for teaching the basics, for encouraging those who enquire and those who long and desire to know more about the Christian faith. So often people say that the last time they really received any systematic and sustained instruction in the Christian faith was during their confirmation classes, and that can be a very long time ago! We need to be much more alert to the opportunities and possibilities which are before us and indeed more alert to the desire for learning.

3. Care and Service. There is a clear gospel mandate for Christian care and service. From what I have seen on the deanery visits, the diocese need not be ashamed or apologetic about its involvement in 'loving and serving the Lord' in the wider community. Very many parishes are involved in a variety of ways, as indeed are very many of our church members, in some form of what may be termed care and service both within the Church and beyond it. Here is an aspect of our life where most clearly we are working alongside other Churches and denominations, other groups and individuals from statutory services and voluntary bodies.

These then are the three priority areas as we look forward and ahead, but what about the matter of how? In other words, we need to address the question of resources in terms of people, finance and buildings, and it is undoubtedly in this area that hard decisions will have to be made, indeed are already having to be made, for it is quite clear to me that there is no way in which we can spend more money than we can actually afford.

I very much hope that deaneries and areas will be fully involved in the discussion and planning for the deployment and financing of resources in terms of those who are ordained and fully stipendiary. I believe we need to look afresh at how best and more effectively we can deploy not only stipendiary persons but also the other varied resources we have at our disposal, ordained and lay; we must work towards an altogether more collaborative and flexible style of ministry.

There is no doubt in my own mind that over the next ten years the diocese ought to be aiming for self-sufficiency in terms of meeting the costs of stipendiary ministers, and that we need to be beginning to put this process into action now.

In matters of finance generally there needs to be a far greater openness and transparency with regard to money within the diocese, what we actually have, where it comes from, how it is spent. Further, we need to be doing much more work on developing a budget strategy which takes a more severely realistic view of things and which reflects more evidently our priorities in mission.

Linked with 'people' in terms of the Church's mission are places, buildings, many of them still in crucial positions strategically but many more in quite the wrong place. I have seen, and been greatly encouraged by, the enterprising and positive schemes of restoration, re-ordering and re-shaping which have taken place in quite a number of our church buildings. I am quite convinced that our church centres of the future must become places for worship, for teaching and for assembly – this last covering a variety of possibilities.

We need urgently to undertake a survey of what buildings we have and what state the buildings are in, how important they are from a heritage point of view, for example. Only having this more detailed information can we hope to begin to move forward in making decisions about how many buildings we need, where they should be, perhaps what new buildings need to be undertaken in quite new places. A first-rate example of what I am talking about was set before me when on one deanery visit I was shown seven huge churches in the space of one square mile; the local churches, their clergy and people were reasonably clear about what ideally they would like to see for the future – the question that needs to be addressed is how we work carefully, creatively and positively from where we are now to where, under God, we believe we ought to be.

I very much hope that 'Agenda for Action' will provide the diocese with the means by which together we can move forward with a vision of life, hope and expectation for the Church of God in London. We need a Church which is vibrant and lively in faith, a Church which by the very nature of its presence, its being and its living is able to make a positive contribution to the spiritual and moral well-being of the capital city – a Church in which together we should be sparing no effort to make fast with bonds of peace the unity which the Spirit gives and all the time seeking to be faithful to the fulfilling of the Saviour's own desire and longing that all may have life and have it in abundance.

22

Looking to the Future*

For God's temple is holy, and that temple you are. (1 Corinthians 3:17)

Recently, I received a copy of 'Concrete Quarterly'. It is not the usual kind of publication that comes across a bishop's desk, and I am still not quite sure why the British Cement Association should send their magazine to the Bishop of London! But with this bishop they certainly found a keenly interested party, for I was brought up very much in the context of builders and buildings. My father and grandfather were both master builders with a small, but I like to think distinctive and quality, family firm, and the builders' yard which surrounded our home formed the backdrop for my early years.

Many of the things that I learnt as I went around with my father have stuck with me and I often find myself making comments to clergy about the state of their buildings, no doubt greatly to their irritation. In fact, I once overheard one of them muttering behind my back, 'you would never think he had not been an archdeacon, would you?'.

For God's temple is holy, and that temple you are.

As my text from St Paul's letter to the Corinthians reminds us, 'church' is as much about ourselves, a people holy to the Lord, as it is about the holy place. Holy people and holy places are bonded and bound together, and there must be a

*Silver Jubilee of Dedication, All Saints with St John, Clifton, Wednesday 1 July 1992

consonancy and an integrity between the two, for 'God's temple is holy, and that temple you are'.

What then are the characteristics for which we should be looking as we reflect upon who and what we are as a people conformed to the dying and rising of Christ, a people called to be holy to the Lord? Holiness of life has consistently featured as one of the great themes of the catholic revival and the catholic movement in our Church. It is certainly a high sounding phrase and one which is much bandied about. But how do we flesh it out? Wherein does this holiness of life consist? I would suggest three areas for our reflection – perseverance in prayer, commitment to catholicity and energy for evangelism.

At the heart of the catholic renewal was the centrality of the eucharist with the desire for the worshipping of God in the beauty of holiness. Those early struggles about the wearing of vestments, the use of candles on the holy table, the reservation of the sacrament and so on were never intended to become struggles simply about the sanctuary and its ornamentation. Rather these were the very means, the outward and visible signs and symbols, of the inwardness of the holy mysteries which would lead the worshipper more deeply and more fully into the death and resurrection of the Saviour, thereby enabling us truly to live his risen life in every aspect of our lives day by day. The sacrificial aspect of the eucharist was reflected in sacrificial living – a simplicity and rule of life, lives lived out of love for God and others. We need urgently, I believe, to recover that perseverance in prayer out of which sprung much which was so attractive and compelling. There is the need for a new asceticism, for a more definite commitment to that *cantus firmus* of prayer daily. Of course, from time to time we shall be inconvenienced, especially if we try to fit our Christian discipleship around everything else which increasingly crowds in upon us and claims our time. We need clear priorities in terms of perseverance in prayer; I am thinking of prayer daily, regular presence at the holy eucharist and the sacrament of penance and reconciliation, the deep, reflective reading of holy scripture. We need a commitment, in short, to all that which is the very stuff of Christian living, of holiness of life. It is a matter of life or death that we do actually make these things a prime concern. It is no use reading about them, talking about them, sharing about them. We need actually to get down on our knees and do something about it – in the words of the New Testament, 'watch and pray'.

God's temple is holy, and that temple you are.

Commitment to catholicism may sound like a party slogan. In fact in their commitment to catholicity our forebears in the catholic revival sought the same as the Reformers themselves, namely to ensure that what obtained in the Church of England was consonant with the Church from the beginning and down the ages, and with the Church worldwide. It is clearly recognised that the Church of England is not just a sect or indeed a somewhat vague collection of diverse congregations. We need ourselves, just as much as anyone else, to beware of that creeping but insidious congregationalism. Rather, we are part of the one holy catholic and apostolic Church. Furthermore, when people say to me, 'well, you can be C of E and believe anything you like or nothing at all', I reply very clearly that we do have our foundational documents. We have our clearly established norms – we profess the faith of the Church, uniquely revealed in the holy scriptures which is set forth in the catholic creeds and borne witness to in the Thirty-Nine Articles of Religion, the Book of Common Prayer and the Ordering of Bishops, Priests and Deacons. Perhaps the saintly Bishop of Winchester, Lancelot Andrewes, encapsulated it rather better when he wrote: 'One Canon . . . two Testaments, three Creeds, four General Councils, five Centuries and the series of the Fathers in that period . . . determine the boundary of our Faith.' Or, again, Bishop Jewell in his *Apologia*, perhaps one of the earliest essays in Anglican self-understanding, when he wrote: 'We have returned to the Apostles and the old catholic fathers. We have planted no new religion, but only have preserved the old that was undoubtedly founded and used by the Apostles of Christ and other holy fathers of the primitive church.' He insisted that 'this lawful reformation . . . is so far from taking us from the name or nature of true Catholics . . . or depriving us of the fellowship of the Apostolic church or impairing the right

Faith, Sacraments, Priesthood and governance of the Catholic Church that it hath cleared and settled them on us'. Such is the basis of our Anglican inheritance – a basis and self-understanding which urgently we need to recover in these days, and we are the ones who should be doing something about it, not from Roman Catholic and other sources, but rather from within the rich treasure-house of our own English tradition.

God's temple is holy, and that temple you are.

It must surely be evident that from the firm foundation of perseverance in prayer and a commitment to catholicity there emerges the energy for evangelism, that indefatigable and indomitable zeal for the winning of souls for Christ. It was not simply the great priestly names of the catholic revival who drew many ordinary women and men to a love for the Lord Jesus Christ and a deeper care and compassion for each other; it was as much the contribution of the laity. The energy for evangelism, for going out and loving and serving the Lord in his world, is the responsibility of each and every one of us. The trouble is that so often we take our faith, and all that our Church offers us, so much for granted. Our business is to make Christ known and that can and does only happen in and through each of us taking a responsibility for evangelism, an evangelism which will be winning as much through who and what we are and the attractiveness of our lives and lifestyle as individuals and as a Church, as it will by our actual invitation to others to 'come and see' – yet such invitations are important and necessary.

Here then, I believe, is our agenda for the future – a future which is always unsure and uncertain, and which therefore means the more urgently that we as individuals and as a Church address ourselves seriously, steadfastly, courteously, and vigorously to these aspects of our life and living in the one holy catholic and apostolic Church: perseverance in prayer, commitment to catholicity, and dedication to making Christ known to all people. Or, as one writer has recently put it, it is a matter 'of ourselves so following in the way of Christ that others find it possible to follow too'. Such was the simple and straightforward gospel of our forebears in the catholic revival. It is equally appropriate and timely for us today.

23

Christian Witness Today*

Unless a grain of wheat falls into the earth and dies, it remains alone; but if it dies, it bears much fruit. (John 12:24)

Cyprian of Carthage is one of the great names in the early history of the Church. He was a person of considerable learning, highly respected, and, from what we can glean of his way of life, he was wealthy – he had considerable landed property, his gardens in Carthage were spacious and beautiful, and his home was a villa of considerable proportions with frescoed walls, gilded ceilings and marble lined rooms. This cultured and luxurious lifestyle was to change dramatically as in mid-life he joined the catechumenate and was baptised into the Christian faith. Soon after his initiation he became priest, and when, shortly after that, a successor to Bishop Donatus was being sought, the overwhelming popular choice to succeed him was Cyprian. He declined, conscious of his inexperience in the Christian faith, let alone in the presbyterate. He hid himself away in his home, but the crowd surrounded it and thronged the avenues around the house. There was no means of escape. The crowd persisted until, reluctantly and fearfully, Cyprian gave his consent to be Bishop of Carthage.

The Church in North Africa was populous and influential. However, as with any group which takes things too much for granted, it had become somewhat stagnant and was much in need of reform and new energy. It was precisely the gifts needed to re-awaken the Church to its witness and its mission which so many recognised in Cyprian and which led him so unwillingly to episcopal ordination. His leadership became

*St Cyprian's, Clarence Gate, Sunday 13 September 1992

crucial, as within hardly any time at all the Decian per-
secution had come upon the Church. This was a time of trial
and testing which was to stretch even the faith of the most
tenacious believers. It was the age of the martyrs, when many
Christians were tortured, imprisoned and executed because
they refused the grains of incense offered to the gods of the
empire.

While such a time seems very far distant from our own,
nevertheless it has to be said that not a lot seems to have
changed with the passage of the years.

Unless a grain of wheat falls into the earth and dies, it
remains alone; but if it dies, it bears much fruit.

Already I have hinted that at the time of Cyprian's appear-
ance on the scene the Church of North Africa had become
self-satisfied and stagnant. Having settled into conformity to
the things of this world, it had come to have little effect in
transforming the hearts, minds and lives of those it would
seek to draw to Christ. The coming of Cyprian saw new
impetus given to instruction and teaching, to apologetic and
the renewal of the life of Church, both clergy and laity. The
situation in our own Church today is not altogether dissimilar.
The Decade of Evangelism, while such a title may not be
particularly appealing, is largely, I believe, about the renewal
of the life of the Church inwardly and spiritually – the renewing of the roots of our own Anglican tradition so that all may
be the more effectively engaged for witness and for mission. Of
course this means that we need new programmes of Christian
catechesis and exegesis, so that we are all able to appreciate
more deeply the truth of the faith, are able to give a reason
for the faith that is in us, and are able to live out the demands
and the privileges of Christian discipleship day by day.

For Christian believing is nothing if it does not issue in the
practicality of Christian witness and mission day by day. Our
faith is not only for Sunday. Rather, as many of the early
writers remind us, the sacramental celebration of Sunday, the
glory, praise and adoration of God on the first day of the
week, is the norm for each and every day of the following
week. We must remember that it is mainly by the people we
are, both individually and together as church, that others will

either be attracted or repelled. The question before us is whether the fruits of the Spirit – long suffering patience, meekness, kindness, gentleness, and not least, charity – are part and parcel of what each of us is individually and what all of us are together; these are qualities and values which are cherished not just as ends in themselves, but which spring from our being together and our sharing together in holy communion. In other words, are we truly striving to grow in grace and in the love of God? Is this a real priority for each of us?

Unless a grain of wheat falls into the earth and dies, it remains alone; but if it dies, it bears much fruit.

Another aspect of the life of the Church of the third century and that of our own is the clear existence of difference and diversity – about a whole range of issues. Throughout Cyprian's ministry as a bishop, much of his time and energy in speaking and in writing is given to doing all in his power to ensure that, in the most difficult and fraught circumstances, the unity of the Church is preserved. If he thought someone was wrong, even the Pope of Rome, Stephen, with whom he had extensive exchanges on the subject of re-baptism, he told them so in no uncertain terms. Differences could often be bitter; virulent verbal exchanges were nothing compared to the physical blows which often passed between opposing parties and groups. Nevertheless, Cyprian worked tenaciously to keep the Christian community together. One of his most important contributions to Christian thinking and literature is his treatise on the unity of the Church. 'There is one Church', he writes, 'which outspreads itself into a multitude of churches, wider and wider in ever increasing fruitfulness; just as the sun has many rays but only one light, and a tree many branches yet only one heart, based in the clinging root, . . . so too the Church flooded with the light of the Lord flings rays over the whole world. Yet it is one light which defuses itself everywhere; the unity of the body knows no partition.' Yet it is not just the unity of the Church which is at stake for Cyprian. The unity of the Church is not an end in itself, but rather it is the model of that which God wills for his entire created order – 'the unity of humanity within itself and with God is that in which alone salvation consists'.

There is an equal concern for unity in our own Church in these days. We face considerable difference and diversity. Committed Christians have profound differences of view across a range of issues from faith and order, sex and sexuality to approaches to those of other faith. Yet it is my firm conviction that even where profound differences of view exist we need all the time to be seeking to deepen the unity which is ours not by right, but by grace alone. I mean that unity which the Spirit gives and which enables us still to love, honour and respect each other even when we have very real disagreements. Too many people are too ready to consign their fellow sisters and brothers in Christ to the eternal bonfire simply because they consider them to fail their test of being a real Christian, a real catholic or whatever. In the final analysis, *the* test, thank God, is altogether more simple and direct. It is minding our own business rather than other people's, it is following in the way of the cross so that others might find it possible to follow too. The way of unity is certainly the way of the cross.

Unless a grain of wheat falls into the earth and dies, it remains alone; but if it dies, it bears much fruit.

Cyprian's condemnation to death was brief and clear. Four simple questions were put to him; and he was found guilty of antagonism to the gods of Rome and to their sacred observances. In the way of many of his faithful people, the bishop was sentenced and beheaded. So Cyprian, Bishop of Carthage, who himself had written of this baptism by blood 'wherein angels are the baptizers, and in which God and his Christ are joyful – the baptism after which no one sins', now sheds his blood for the sake of his Lord. It was truly the age of the martyrs.

However, we need equally to recognise that the twentieth century is no less an age of the martyrs than those early years. I can recall how on the occasion of Pope John Paul's visit to England, one of the most moving moments was when Archbishop Robert Runcie and the Pope knelt and prayed together in the chapel in Canterbury Cathedral dedicated to the martyrs of the twentieth century. Whilst we ourselves may not yet be called to testify to our faith to the point of shedding our blood, nevertheless we are equally called to be martyrs and witnesses to the risen and living Lord Jesus Christ in his Church, in his world and in our own lives today.

The martyrdom to which we are called makes costly demands upon us for change and growth if we are not simply to be conformed to the things of this world but caught up in the transforming power of the Holy Spirit. The Spirit is at work in us to draw us more deeply and more perfectly into that fulness of being which Christ wills for all humanity, for the entire created order. Here then is but the beginning and the continuing of a process by which God will bring us also to that place where blessed Cyprian together with the whole company of heaven rejoice forever in God's presence and glory.

24

The City of God*

The wise man built his house on the rock. The rain fell, the floods came and the winds blew and beat against that house; yet it did not fall, because it had its foundation on the rock. (Matthew 7:24, 25)

Many buildings have been and gone. At the present time there is a good deal of talk about the demolition of buildings hardly fifty years old, which when they were built were hailed as the latest and the best. Buildings disappear for many and varied reasons, and not just because of storm and tempest, as scripture puts it, or 'Acts of God', as the insurers would have it. Indeed, in the square mile of the City of London the great fire in the seventeenth century put paid to most of what had been. Yet the ever changing style and landscape of any city is, or ought to be, a subtle movement which, in cherishing and nourishing the past, offers possibility and potential for the present and the future.

The 'city' is a central theme in the record of God's dealings with his people, a theme which is focused more particularly in Jerusalem. The history of this particular city stretches back, some would argue, into the fourteenth chapter of the Book of Genesis – the place from whence the strange and enigmatic figure Melchizedek emerges. As a city it had already had many siege-works raised against it. It had fallen prey to marauding groups and mighty armies. Yet somehow or another out of the rubble and ruins it had emerged once more. Throughout the Davidic reign it symbolised the greatness of God's power, it celebrated the unique and distinctive

*Patronal Festival, St Margaret Lothbury, Tuesday 28 July 1992

privilege of God's people as a chosen nation, a holy people.
It rose to a pre-eminent place as the city of the great king –
'walk about Zion, go round about her; and tell the towers
thereof. Mark well her bulwarks, set up her houses that ye
may tell them that come after' (Psalm 48).

This is typical of many of the biblical references to the
splendour and grandeur of the place. In Jerusalem all the
highest of the people's aspirations are focused. Its elegant
and massive buildings are described in considerable detail,
together with their furnishing and decoration. No wonder it
was the joy of the whole earth. Indeed, so impressive is this
city that the scriptures describe the hereafter in terms modelled upon the earthly Jerusalem – 'and I saw the new
Jerusalem . . .' (Revelation 21:2).

Yet this is not the only or the enduring picture that we
have of Jerusalem. In stark contrast, the Lamentations of
Jeremiah describe in movingly poetic form the utter destruction which came upon this city in the year 587 either on the
seventh or tenth day of the fifth month of that year – the year
when the mighty Babylonian armies destroyed Jerusalem and
its temple and deported its population leaving only the poor-
est and the weakest.

> How lowly sits the city that was full of people – how like
> a widow has she become, she that was great among the
> nations! She that was a princess among the cities has
> become a vassal . . . how the gold has grown dim, how the
> pure gold is changed! All her people yearn as they search
> for bread . . . in the dust of the streets lie the young and
> the old . . . .
>
> (Lamentations 1:1ff)

The Lament over the devastated city describes in clear detail
the utter destruction which has come upon Jerusalem.

I believe that it is not only Jerusalem of which scripture is
speaking. This particular city serves as a model for all our
cities, towns, villages and human communities. For on the
one hand, it can be said that the purposes of God for all
people are portrayed as to be achieved in the coming city of
God, and to that extent our earthly cities are, or ought to be,

something of a foretaste of the heavenly city. Yet on the other hand, it has to be recognised that the city is a place in which that which is evil, oppressive and depraved in human life can find its most intense expression. Within a city, too, there are to be found the highest achievements of man's creativity, imagination, co-operation and industry, existing side by side with the results of man's self-centredness, wickedness and greed.

The bible, then, sets before us this paradox. It is a paradox seen in any city, and surely it must be the duty of every citizen always to seek that abundance of life which our Lord and Saviour Jesus Christ wills for all.

Having said that, we need always to recognise that places are as good or as bad as the people who comprise them. In the first place it was 'citizenship' which defined city, not the buildings. And any dictionary definition will describe 'city' as 'a collective body of inhabitants . . . a community of people'. So what of us today? Where is our place? What is our contribution?

It is interesting that it is often in the small things, in those little and unsuspecting ways, that great things can actually be effected – take, for example, the parable of the mustard seed. Often it can appear that the issues are so enormous and complex that there is little that each of us as individuals can do or say to influence 'them' – the decision-makers, those concerned about transport, environment, construction and so on. Thus individual responsibility and accountability wanes, and we are the poorer for that. It is, I think, typified in the prevalent attitude to litter; an unwanted bit of paper is discarded quite unthinkingly – we all do it at sometime or another, and we reckon that 'they' will see to it, sweep it up, clear it away. It is perhaps a small and trivial example but it is symptomatic of trends in our society, of abrogation of a sense of personal responsibility and accountability, which lead inevitably to the sort of situation which provokes Jeremiah's Lament.

In a similar vein, I remember as a youngster that everyone in our street took responsibility for their own 'front'. No matter how you were placed, it still did not stop you from sweeping the front and keeping things neat and tidy, and contributing to the general tidiness of the street as a whole. Again, perhaps this is a somewhat trivial example but it is one of those small things which in the end do make a very considerable difference. I am talking about the recovery among us of what I would call civic pride. Each of us must make our own particular contribution, we must recognise that we are members one of another and that we do have a responsibility one towards another for the good and well-being of the whole. There is much talk these days about quality of life. In the final analysis, as scripture so rightly reminds us, quality of life has as much to do with the disposition of the heart, our attitude and our priorities Godwards and therefore our love and service to our neighbour, as it has to do with the planners and the builders.

The wise man built his house on the rock. The rain fell, the floods came and the winds blew and beat against that house; yet it did not fall, because it had its foundations on the rock.

It may seem that I have strayed far from this text. I hope I have not, for it must surely have become evident that if indeed a city is to become the joy of the whole earth, then the lives of its citizens are to be built upon rock – the sure and certain rock of faith is our Lord and Saviour Jesus Christ who is the same yesterday, today and forever. Christian principles, insights and values have informed the way of life of many faithful citizens down the ages. If such principles, insights and values are to be sustained in our present time, then our contribution individually, and our contribution collectively as a Church, calls for a martyrdom in terms of our own being, lives and lifestyle, so that indeed, founded on that rock who is Jesus Christ, the cities of this world may begin to be altogether more realistic and effective signs of that city which is to come – the city which has foundations, whose builder and maker is God; that city which will have no need of sun or moon to shine upon it, for the glory of God is its light and its lamp is the lamb.

My hope is that we will each be more certain of our own vocation and calling as citizens both of earth and of heaven;

and that we see to it that we do all we can to effect the coming of God's kingdom here and now, as it is in heaven.

25

Living Stones*

You also, as living stones, must be built up into a spiritual temple, and form a holy priesthood to offer spiritual sacrifices acceptable to God through Jesus Christ. (1 Peter 2:5)

Bare Ruined Choirs is the title of a magisterial book by David Knowles, the distinguished historian of the English monasteries. One place mentioned in the book is Rievaulx Abbey, just a little distance from Helmsley in North Yorkshire. It has, and always has had, an extraordinary fascination for me personally ever since I first visited those bare, ruined choirs. It is set in a magnificent position – a large, wooded river valley – and even as you walk around today, you can almost see, hear and experience the life of worship and dedicated service offered to God by literally hundreds of monks who had given themselves and their lives to his glory.

It may seem rather odd that a building in ruins can wield so much power over the human heart and mind. But the fact is that stones such as these – discarded remnants of a bygone age though they might appear – can bring the past to life in a compelling and immediate way. The ruins of any great structure, as well as being a fruitful source for the historian and archaeologist, can so often awaken our curiosity and inspire our imagination. What sort of people might have once walked and talked here? What times of joy and sorrow might they have known? What dreams and desires might they have nurtured? How might their earthly pilgrimage have drawn to its close? In a real sense, then, the ruins of Rievaulx are not

*Service of Thanksgiving for the Conservation of the Old Church, St John, Great Stanmore, Friday 17 July 1992

fossilised remains but *living stones*, silent witnesses to the human story through the passage of time.

The stones of Great Stanmore Old Church could doubtless tell many stories of the life and times of this corner of Middlesex throughout the last three centuries. Pevsner describes the ruins as one of Middlesex's best, due in part, no doubt, to the skill and craftsmanship of Nicholas Stone, the mastermason to the Crown who is known to have worked on parts of the building. It is a little unnerving to think that William Laud, one of my predecessors as Bishop of London, lost his head, amongst other things, for consecrating the building for public worship some three hundred and sixty years ago. The charge against him was that he 'outwent Popery in the consecration of chapels' – and particular mention was made of this place in that charge. I do not know whether a service of thanksgiving for the completion of conservation repairs could be held against me in quite the same way, but I fully intend keeping my head for some time to come!

We can, then, be thankful that the appeal has so successfully conserved the ruins for future generations to love and enjoy, enabling the building to continue to be an attractive feature of the local environment as well as being a rich mine for the historian and archaeologist. But I hope that it will be as *living stones* that the ruins of the church will exercise their greatest power. How might this be?

St Peter was a man fired with enthusiasm for the growth and extension of the Church. He had witnessed an explosive response to the preaching of the good news of Jesus Christ that he and his fellow apostles had undertaken on their missionary journeys. As he sought to build up the Church in word as well as deed he wrote in his first letters to one of the infant Christian communities of the need for those new to the faith to be knit together like stones in a building: 'You also, as living stones, must be built up into a spiritual temple, and form a holy priesthood to offer spiritual sacrifices acceptable to God through Jesus Christ.' Peter recognised that stones have remarkable qualities and he set out to encourage his fellow Christians to adopt these characteristics for themselves. So what are the marks of a living stone?

The resilience of many of our older buildings through centuries of subjection to the elements is a testimony to the enduring strength of stone. Stone has a remarkable capacity to remain *firm* through the passage of time, and just as a building relies on the firmness of its stones to support it in adverse weather, so Christians need to be firm in their faith if they are to remain steadfast in life's adversities. The strength of the Christian tradition, in its sacraments and scriptures, in its worship and prayer, is more than sufficient to keep us sturdy and steadfast in the storms of life if only we would draw more deeply and determinedly upon it. And that will require a greater rigour and discipline in our discipleship than we normally manage to muster.

But even the strongest stone structure needs to be *flexible* if it is to remain upright. If you try standing on top of a tower block in a storm, you will quickly appreciate that unless the structure was able to bend it could never survive. Consequently, a Christian's life and worship will not be unthinkingly dogmatic and rigid but responsive to the needs and conditions of the society in which he finds himself. That does not mean, to quote St Paul, getting 'tossed back and forth by the waves and blown here and there by every wind of doctrine'. But it does mean the ability, which has marked the Christian Church throughout its life, to adapt and change in response to local circumstances. So, living stones will be *firm* and *flexible*.

> You also, as living stones, must be built up into a spiritual temple, and form a holy priesthood to offer spiritual sacrifices acceptable to God through Jesus Christ.

One of the awe-inspiring things about our cathedrals and churches is the way they have been hallowed by prayer over centuries. The daily round of morning and evening prayer, the offering of the eucharist, the personal prayers of the visitor or pilgrim, all beat against the stonework. Our most inspiring places of worship are most often those which reflect the action of the life of prayer upon them. So the life of a living stone will be one marked by persistence in prayer and that discipline will leave a visible mark on the individual concerned: a life not susceptible to the transient conflicts and emotions

of this world but stable and secure in a foundation built upon
the solid rock that is Christ.

But these lives will not be so other-worldly that they
obscure their essentially *human* quality and character. Like the
saints of God who have made most impact on the Christian
tradition they will be robust and resilient individuals who
have learned to be honest about the fragility and frailty of
their human nature – rough-hewn stones, not finely polished
marble. They will not run away from the demands and challenges of life into the easy security of the sanctuary, so heaven-
ly-minded that they are of no earthly use. Rather they will
embrace, love and identify with the world in order to bring
the grace and power of the Lord into it and upon it. So, living
stones who will be *holy* yet *human*.

> You also, as living stones, must be built up into a spiritual
> temple, and form a holy priesthood to offer spiritual sacri-
> fices acceptable to God through Jesus Christ.

Perhaps the most obvious mark of stone structures that
Peter had in mind when trying to teach his infant Christian
communities was their *dependence*. Unless stones sit closely and
tightly together in a building the structure will soon prove
unstable and collapse. The art of the stonemason can be to
place very different stones side by side that through balance
and gravity enable a building to stand the test of time. Christians can discover this in their life together as they trust and
depend on one another, as they grow in courtesy and respect
for their brothers and sisters in the faith who may be from
very different and diverse backgrounds. By prayer and fellowship we ought to become secure and stable supports for one
another, especially in times of crisis and difficulty. No Christian can be a living stone and remain alone.

But while the stones of any structure depend and lean upon
one another they do not remain static and stationary. In
Westminster Abbey the art of those soaring arches is their
ability to sweep our eyes heavenward, each stone combining
with its neighbour to send a pillar here or a buttress there.
And here, of course, lies the *dynamic* quality of the Christian
Church for our life of mutual dependence ought not to leave
us simply preoccupied with those within the holy temple.

Rather the Church should be a divine society reaching out-
wards and upwards. It is when we become content simply
with trying to prop each other up that the Church finds itself
self-obsessed and introspective. Rather we must learn to carry
this dynamic perspective into our mission and evangelism,
reaching boldly into the community around us with hearts
willing to serve the needs of our neighbours – our eyes kept
on heaven as we seek to transform and change the world.

So Christians called to be living stones – characterised by
their firmness and flexibility, their holiness and humanity,
their dependency and dynamism – are challenged to a construction project altogether more exciting and adventurous
than any property developer might conceive. We can be
thankful that the stones of ruins speak to us of our own
vocation to be living stones, but they also contain a sober
reminder of what can happen to the Church of God when it
ceases to live the life of faith to the full. So, since we have
accepted Christ Jesus as Lord, let us live in union with him.
Let us be rooted in him, built in him, grow strong in the
faith; let our hearts overflow with thankfulness and we will
see ourselves as living stones built up into a spiritual temple,
offering spiritual sacrifices acceptable to God through Jesus
Christ.

26

Working Together*

That they may all be one . . . so that the world may believe. (John 17:20)

Some two hundred and fifty years ago John Wesley made his first incursion into my former Diocese of Wakefield. He approached Huddersfield from the west, from across the Pennines, and he subsequently wrote in his journal, 'I rode over the mountains to Huddersfield, a wilder people I never saw in England. The men, women and children filled the streets as we rode along and seemed just ready to devour us'. Fortunately, they did not devour him, and I am sure that if the same John Wesley were to make the same journey today he would write somewhat differently – at least I hope he would!

He would surely note the very good ecumenical relationships which the Church leaders and others in those parts have developed over a comparatively short period of time. The success of those relationships has been in no small measure due to the first chairman of the ecumenical council in those parts, a Methodist Chairman of District. He it was who encouraged us in our meeting together with a first priority simply to talk with and among each other as fellow Christians, to worship and pray together, to share silence together, to exchange our thoughts and reflections as those who, in our respective denominations, had been entrusted with ministerial leadership. It may seem very obvious indeed, but we were being encouraged to savour and to enjoy each other's company, to be what our Lord had exhorted his disciples to be – friends together, 'to love one another as I have loved you'

*Wesley's Chapel, City Road, Sunday 19 January 1992

(John 15:12). We are all on the same journey, a journey of faith where there is both knowing and unknowing, a journey which implies risk and launching out into the deep – a discipleship which is as exciting as it is daunting.

So whilst it might appear to be somewhat obvious and may be even simplistic, I think we do need to remind ourselves that in the ecumenical process our relationships one with another across our respective denominations are as much as anything nurtured and encouraged by Christian friendship. It is not just a friendship which is conveniently contrived for the purposes of putting on a good face in the interests of Christian unity. It is a friendship which is rooted and grounded in that quality of love about which St Paul rhapsodises in 1 Corinthians 13 – a love which is patient and kind, a love which is not arrogant or rude, which does not insist on its own way; in short, a love which bears all things, believes all things, hopes all things, endures all things. It is a friendship which, so rooted and grounded in Christ, does not simply break apart when difference and disagreement is encountered, but rather is sufficiently resilient to enable friends to sit down and explore in depth, in sincerity and with real respect and courtesy, those things which continue to keep us apart. So let us not either decry or despise the networks of denominational friendships which we have and in which we rejoice. Rather let us seek ways in which these can be nourished, strengthened and deepened.

That they may all be one . . . so that the world may believe.

A not entirely unconnected theme in the New Testmaent is that of communion or koinonia – that fellowship of the things we have in common and in which we participate through the amazing grace given us in the death and resurrection of Jesus now made present to us and effected for us in the power of the Holy Spirit. There is much which binds us together in spite of ourselves. We share a common baptism into the one Lord and Saviour Jesus Christ; we share the holy scriptures, the Word of God which is sharper than a two-edged sword discerning the thoughts and intentions of the heart, the Word of God which is publicly proclaimed, taught, preached, reflected upon and taken into our thoughts and prayers, the Word which shapes our lives, life and lifestyle; we share times of prayer and praise, times of anguish and sorrow; we share a common calling to the Church to go forth and make disciples, to go into the world to proclaim Christ crucified and risen and the abundance of life which he wills for all people – a call both to ministry and to service together. This sharing of so much must surely be the context of our celebrations together in the communion and fellowship of the universal Church. This must be the context, too, of our approach to those matters of faith and order which as yet sadly and painfully keep us apart and at which we need steadfastly to keep working and praying.

So just where are our ecumenical endeavours taking us? Of one thing I am quite certain and that is that ecumenism is very much about renewing and celebrating the roots of our own distinctive inheritance either as Methodists, Anglicans, Baptists, Pentecostalists or whatever. It is about the continuing quest on the part of us all for that which so preoccupied John Wesley and which is so much reflected in his writings – scriptural holiness. It is not irrelevant, I think, to note that the three works which so formed his own mind in this matter were Thomas à Kempis' *Imitation of Christ*, Jeremy Taylor's *Holy Living and Holy Dying*, and William Law's *A Serious Call to the Devout and Holy Life*. Wesley wrote that these works 'so convinced me more than ever of the absolute impossibility of being half a Christian'. He declared that as a consequence 'the light flowed in so mightily upon my soul that everything appeared in a new view'. There is much talk about holiness of life, about the call to be holy which, if we are not careful, simply results in a more intensive form of religiosity. The quest for scriptural holiness is a quest in penitence and in faith for a discipline of life and living which gives a real priority to our prayer and our reflection upon the holy scriptures; a priority to word and sacrament; to allowing the mind of Christ so to be formed in us that we are no longer conformed to the things of this world but rather, in the transforming power of the Spirit, our lives are lived to God's praise and glory and in service of others. It is the call in these days of busy-ness, frenzy and rush to stop, to look and to listen, to have the courage to carve out a 'quiet time', as our evangelical forebears called it, so that in the midst of the day's round we can be still and hear what the Lord God is saying to us in the depths of our heart. It is the courage to pay attention to what Wesley calls 'the kingdom of an inward heaven' and in so doing he picks up one of the earliest and most consistent themes of the Christian spiritual tradition about paying heed to ourselves, of the need for stillness, silence and that deep inward openness to God, so that God may continue his work of renewal and transformation in us, so that no longer it is I who live but Christ who lives in me. So far as our pilgrimage together ecumenically is concerned, it means that at a time when perhaps we are not able to discern particular initiatives or dramatic ways forward, that we do remain faithful to the Lord and to each other in the sure and certain knowledge that when our own endeavours seem to be stumbling, he remains with us, leading us onwards and forwards, and our chief business is to grow together and become more trusting of each other and indeed more trusting of the power and purposes of God himself.

That they may all be one . . . so that the world may believe.

But then let us not belittle the very considerable distance we have already travelled and the huge advances in a whole variety of ways which have been made ecumenically. Let us not despise either the very considerable number of small and informal networks of Christian people and friends as these are, to my mind, the most encouraging developments. Recently, as I visited one of our deaneries in Brent, I began the day with morning prayers among a group of clergy, presided over by a Roman Catholic lay woman, whose churches form an ecumenical covenant. It was nothing particularly dramatic or exciting, I admit, but from that commitment in prayer together there is the commitment to a very effective ministry, mission and service within the wider community. If such models were replicated more widely the ecumenical scene would be greatly transformed. A day for small things no doubt, wrote the Prophet Zephaniah, but who would dare despise it?

It is, I suspect, in the small things that our life together can and will grow. The major thrust at the present time, so far as things ecumenical are concerned, is less an initiative from above than the encouragement of local partnership and growth, and not least, in this Decade of Evangelism, a deep engagement together in ministry, mission and service to the wider community. Shortly before Christmas I was present at St Martin-in-the-Fields to commemorate Shelter's twenty-fifth birthday. The church was packed with people from every conceivable denomination, and it was the homeless that had brought us together. We had not had to think denominationally – we had each come together out of our Christian care and concern. There are many other examples of the way in which, paradoxically, the world has been the catalyst for the Church's own gospel.

In practically every ecumenical context there is the exhortation for all Christian people to engage together except in those things which in conscience particular individuals or churches feel they cannot. This still, I believe, holds good, and we must certainly give proper respect and space to such conscientious exceptions. Yet we really do need more actively to work together at every level. Such working together does not just happen by itself. It involves all of us, ordained and lay. Each one of us needs to resolve that, in whatever way may seem appropriate for us and however small and insignificant the initiative appears to be, we do begin to engage much more actively in making what we pray for a reality. In the days ahead we must seek every means possible of engaging with Christians of other denominations in bringing the truth of the gospel to a world, which perhaps more than ever in these times needs a word of hope, forgiveness, reconciliation and of peace.

27

Return to Romania*

The Lord has comforted his people, he has redeemed Jerusalem.
(Isaiah 52:9)

It was rather late in the day, about seven o'clock in the evening, that I finally made it to Cernavoda. It was well worth the perseverance.

The small delegation which I was leading on behalf of the Archbishop of Canterbury to the Romanian Orthodox Church had been staying at the beautiful and almost heaven-like monastery of Varatec in Moldavia. We had set off early by road with the aim of getting to Galati by lunchtime. It was a long and hot journey, even hotter by the time we had reached Galati. There we were met by the archbishop, a lively, articulate and enthusiastic man, with a number of local representatives. It was also a very great personal pleasure for me to visit at the same time the former archbishop, Antim, who had been a great friend and supporter of the exchange programme between the Church of England and the Romanian Orthodox Church in the early years of the Ceauşescu regime. We then sped through the streets of Galati escorted by the archbishop's car only to reach the ferry just as it was departing! So a detour by road was necessary, making for a further four hours' driving to Cernavoda.

The site of the hospice at Cernavoda stands proudly on a hilltop overlooking the Danube. The building was well up to ground floor level, and, bearing in mind the enormous amount of work in preparing the site and putting in the foundations

*Service of Thanksgiving for the Hospice of St Lawrence in Cernavoda, St Martin-in-the-Fields, Saturday 1 February 1992

and all the lower ground floor service area, it was a very considerable achievement to have got that far so fast. I gather that by now the first children are already at Cernavoda. There was enormous goodwill and enthusiasm locally for the project. There was commitment, co-operation and support in what has been a truly Christian initiative – a Christian initiative which has brought together the gifts, skills, support and enthusiasm of so many people; an initiative which demonstrates that when energies are applied for creative, positive and good purposes rather than destructive, divisive and wicked ones, there is a real flowering and flourishing among a wide variety of people.

The Lord has comforted his people, he has redeemed Jerusalem.

It was good to have the opportunity to return to Romania. In very many ways it was like going home. I have to say I was both shocked and saddened at the state of the capital city, Bucharest – a fine and noble city which, even in the short time I had been there, I had come to know well and hold in very great affection. The despoliation of the Ceauşescu regime was evident in almost every street. Yet even amid such outward and visible devastation and destruction, I was immensely encouraged and heartened by the indomitable spirit of the people. Their persistence and determination not to be ground down, the warmth of their hearts, were as immediately evident as ever. They need our continuing prayer. They need, too, whatever practical aid and support we in the West can give them. We rejoice at the collapse of the regimes of tyranny and fear, but a price has been paid and continues to be paid by those who have endured them and who are now freed from them. A price has to be paid among ourselves as well – that of sharing the many goods and resources which we naturally take so much for granted, those very basic rations and conditions for human life, dignity and well-being.

There is a further project in Albania – again, a quite modest project in what can seem such a hugely impossible task. Our Christian conviction, however, spurs us on. We know from the record of scripture that, in the face of overwhelming odds, we should never despise the small and apparently insignificant; indeed quite the reverse. It is often in the small and the apparently insignificant – the grain of wheat, the mustard seed – that the coming of God's kingdom is to be discerned, his kingdom of peace and love, of justice, righteousness and holiness.

Cernavoda is, I believe, a sign of hope and promise for the future, one of the many such signs which are to be seen not only in Romania but in other places in eastern Europe too. As I reflect upon what has been achieved, I would like to suggest two thoughts in regard to Cernavoda.

The first is that any vision has its excitement and its enthusiasm, but it also needs a sense of realism and the recognition that setbacks and disappointments, frustrations and exasperation will necessarily arise; yet you go on with the enterprise on which you are set out. Here surely is something of a model for us as we continue in our Christian discipleship, fellowship, ministry, mission and service. What matters most is that we continue steadfast and sure in that way along which we believe ourselves to have been called, looking unto Jesus the author and finisher of our faith who for the joy that was set before him despised the shame, endured the cross and is now set down at the right hand of the throne of God.

The Lord has comforted his people, he has redeemed Jerusalem.

Secondly, I rejoice that this work has encouraged a proper partnership between Christians of different Churches, traditions and backgrounds. We have been brought together in that which is basic and fundamental to any Christian ministry – the service of others and love of our neighbour. This was another sign of hope and promise that I witnessed in Romania – again small beginnings perhaps, but a very necessary movement and the way along which I would want to urge the Churches in Romania steadfastly to continue. One of my appointments last July was to visit the Theological Institute in Bucharest where I had lived twenty-five years ago, and where representatives from the World Council of Churches were meeting representatives of the Romanian Orthodox

Church in order to discuss ways forward for co-ordinating more practical ecumenical initiatives. The Churches have a crucial role to play in the rebuilding of that marvellous country and its people, not only in a religious and moral sense, but also in the promoting of a greater toleration and understanding between and among the disparate elements of the people; in recognising, celebrating and building up the varied and distinctive groups to form a social and political unity for the good of all. One of my very happy memories was the occasion when Bishop Nifon and I conducted the inauguration of a joint project between our Church of the Resurrection and the nearby Biserca Icoane – a joint church social community centre. In England our ecumenical endeavours give us much to celebrate, but we need to ensure that we keep working with other denominations and Churches, so that we may indeed together seek to bring that abundance of life which the one Lord and Saviour Jesus Christ wills for all people.

28

Good News to the Poor*

He said therefore, 'What is the kingdom of God like? And to what shall I compare it? It is like a grain of mustard seed which a man took and sowed in his garden; and it grew and became a tree, and the birds of the air made nests in its branches.' And again he said, 'To what shall I compare the kingdom of God? It is like leaven which a woman took and hid in three measures of meal, till it was all leavened.' (Luke 13:18–21)

The involvement of churches in social care and action is obvious to anyone acquainted with Church history. It begins with the life and teaching of Jesus himself and has continued throughout the centuries. That history defends the notion that true Christian faith is involved in all aspects of human life and existence.

I want to stress my basic belief in a faithful and active Church. We are called to be a community of believers who express our love and devotion to the risen and living Lord Jesus Christ not only by what we say but in what we do. In the context of the Decade of Evangelism we need to remind ourselves even more that our task is to proclaim the kingdom of God not only through care and nurture but also through proclamation and service – so says Resolution 44, from the Lambeth Conference of 1988, on Evangelism in the Anglican Communion. An acknowledgement of God's kingdom confirms our love of God, and we show that love by how we respond to our neighbour.

The two parables of the mustard seed and yeast are famous

*Anniversary Celebration for the Shaftesbury Society, St Paul's, Robert Adam Street, Friday 8 November 1991 for their brevity. Jesus had the knack of using everyday images and commodities to explain great and simple truths. Both of these parables are told to remind us that the good news which is at the heart of the gospel can begin in very small, insignificant ways in people's lives; the seed is often sown in the most unlikely and unpromising situations and circumstances. It is our business to see that the seed is planted, that it is actually sown.

The mustard seed grew to become a tree and the birds of the air perched in its branches. The yeast worked its way all through the dough. Both stories show that the seed – a word of life, a caring gesture, an act of kindness – is never sown to no effect. Its potential is enormous and that potential can be realised in a whole variety of ways through God's good grace.

I would like to draw attention to two particular projects in London that started as seeds thanks to the Urban Mission Appeal. I have been most encouraged by the story of Kilburn Evangelical Church and Centre. Dating back almost a hundred years, this church is at the centre of a community which is affected by some of the worst social problems in London. As a result of the Appeal, however, giant strides have been made and a centre for the young homeless is now open for six young people and very soon another six places will be made available. This is a good news story indeed.

Similarly, in Frazer Street, Chiswick, a thriving congregation of more than eighty now worship at the Zoe Christian Fellowship. This mission began its life in 1880 as a ragged school 'dedicated to the poor, from which bread was handed out to the waifs and strays'. In an area affected by poor housing and drug abuse the presence of the Fellowship, backed up by the Urban Mission Appeal, is crucially important.

We can celebrate all that God has given us in such projects, and, as we do so, I would like to focus on two main thoughts. Firstly, we celebrate and proclaim our faith in the God who raised our Lord Jesus Christ from the dead and brought him to glory. Truly Christ is risen; Jesus is Lord. This same Jesus tells us, 'I came that you may have life, life in all its fullness' (John 10:10). But our celebration and proclamation has to be put into practice in Christian service. Often there is far too much talking, and far too little action. Faith in action means expressing God's love for us by doing what we can to bring that fullness of life, which Christ wills and which is at the heart of the gospel, to all – the suffering, the needy, the poor, the homeless. We are called upon to welcome those at the margins, the outcasts, and to enable people to feel part of the Christian family. Jesus often focuses his attention on the dispossessed and those whom society has cast out; hence his use of the passage from the prophet Isaiah to reinforce his message that the day of the Lord had indeed dawned with his coming:

> The Spirit of the Lord is upon me,
> because he has anointed me to preach good news to
>   the poor.
> He has sent me to proclaim release to the captives
> and recovering of sight to the blind,
> to set at liberty those who are oppressed,
> to proclaim the acceptable year of the Lord.
>
> (Luke 4:18–19)

Jesus' message was a message of hope for all, not least for the people who saw themselves as poor, captive, oppressed or rejected. It was a message which from the very beginning the Christian communities and churches seized and acted upon.

I reflected recently, as I was in Istanbul for the enthronement of the new Patriarch of Constantinople, that it was in that very same place over fifteen hundred years ago that one of the most famous of the early Christian writers, St John Chrysostom, Bishop of Constantinople, preached precisely this same message to his own people in these words:

> Consider that Christ is that tramp who comes in need of a night's lodgings. You turn him away and then start laying rugs on the floor, draping the walls, hanging lamps on silver chains on the columns. Meanwhile the tramp is locked up in prison and you never give him a glance. By all means make your house beautiful but also look after the poor or rather look after the poor first. Adorn your house if you

will but do not forget your brother in distress. He is a temple of infinitely greater value.

Secondly, there are no limits to the power of the Holy Spirit. The mustard seed and the yeast are simple examples which remind us of the quite unexpected and unimagined things which can and do happen when we are true to our Christian faith and the living out of it. We can all think of people and situations where God has been able to work far beyond anything we could ever have imagined.

In my former Diocese of Wakefield I launched what became known as the Bishop's Centenary Fund. This was very much a 'faith in action' fund in that it was aimed at helping the Church Urban Fund and financing other projects to help the mission and ministry of the diocese. Our target was one million pounds. Regardless of the marvellous amount of money actually raised, there was a real sense of fun, fellowship and celebration of faith which emerged in the numerous events which we organised and which reminded me that there is always more to such an enterprise than simply money-raising. Money-raising is important, but there is so much else besides.

So, in giving thanks to God, by all means let us proclaim that Christ is risen and Jesus is Lord; that salvation has come among us through God's uncovenanted graciousness in Christ. But this good news is not for keeping for ourselves or to ourselves. We are sent forth and sent out to live his risen life; we whom the Spirit lights, to bring light to others.

29

In the Day of Adversity Consider*

In the day of prosperity be joyful, and in the day of adversity consider. (Ecclesiastes 7:14)

Recently a headline caught my eye: 'England firmly on the path of self-destruction.' Another prediction of the doom and gloom variety, I thought to myself. But what, in fact, was it referring to? The ongoing recession, the blight of terrorism, the human cost of unemployment, or perhaps it was even an abbreviation for the Church of England?

Looking more closely at the newspaper I found that it referred to the unfortunate trials and tribulations of the England cricket team in Sri Lanka. And the reasons given for the cricket team's poor performance? 'Umpiring errors' and 'undetected jerked deliveries'.

There have been rather different 'umpiring errors' and 'jerked deliveries' which have led to a distinct change in mood in the country during the past year. Last April we had a newly elected government and there was a high degree of euphoria in many circles – everything would be all right after all. How things have changed!

Even within the Church of England it has not been an easy year. For some it has been eventful and exciting, a cause of real rejoicing; for others a time of adversity, pain and hurt; certainly a time to consider. Despite the ongoing excellent work of many parishes up and down the country there is a general sense of the need for clarity of vision and purpose. Now, more than at any time in recent years, the Church needs to harness its resources and assess its priorities because

*United Guilds Service, St Paul's Cathedral, Friday 26 March 1993

more and more people are looking to us for spiritual and moral guidance in the complexities and confusions of our day. We need an Agenda for Action.

In the day of prosperity be joyful, and in the day of adversity consider.

Here is sober wisdom from a writer and thinker some two thousand years ago; advice which is both timely and realistic for all of us today. When times are good, of course we can and should be joyful; when we are thriving and successful, when things are going well, there are the outward and visible signs of pleasure, joy and happiness. But when in adversity, whether from recession, unemployment, the never-ending threat of terrorism and violence on our streets, the writer of Ecclesiastes calls upon us 'to consider'. We certainly need to consider when we find ourselves in adverse situations and not simply resign ourselves; we need to think carefully, to contemplate with a spiritual dimension. That is the meaning of the original Hebrew. But what are we to consider? What is it that the author of this Old Testament book is inviting us to contemplate? After all, someone who suggests that the day of death is to be preferred to the day of birth and that sorrow is better than laughter (Ecclesiastes 7:2–3) is not giving us exactly the kind of positive encouragement for which we might be looking in present circumstances!

Perhaps it would be better to join the song of fools than listen to the rebuke of the wise. But, before we dismiss the advice as utterly inappropriate even irrelevant, it would be of benefit to take a closer look at what this particular sage is suggesting to us.

Our writer, as with thinkers and writers in any age, is grappling with the dismaying reality of life – that of our basic human condition. He speaks out of a context of considerable prosperity, and this makes him all the more potent a commentator for our contemporary society. The material and intellectual resources of the ancient world were at his disposal, as were the delights and desires of the flesh. The permissive society is no new invention or experience. Ecclesiastes speaks for humanity. In the words of one commentator: 'We hear the still sad music in his pages, and they will never be out of date – the issues they face so fearlessly are the basic issues of existence which the town dweller in Megalopolis will have to face as surely as the king in Jerusalem.' The city, however you describe it, is a primary clue as to what men and women have made of the basic issue of existence. It is the outward and visible sign of who and what we are as individuals, as a people created, fashioned, made in God's image and likeness. The undergirding principle of our writer's views about life does not emerge until the very last verse of his whole discourse. Yet the last verse is crucial to our understanding not only of this passage but of the whole bible, of our whole existence: 'Fear God, keep his commandments, for this is the whole duty of man.'

It was something at least of this which was the guiding principle in the very foundation of the Guilds and Liveries of the City of London in an attempt to ensure the keeping of God's commandments about standards and justice and right and fair dealing. Gone may be the days when that which did not come up to scratch was publicly denounced as well as the unfortunate offending trader; when the baker might find himself dragged through the streets of London on a cart with the inferior loaf around his neck whilst the crowd looked on both in amusement and contempt. Nevertheless, the imperative remains that if the City of London is to retain its reputation as an attractive, innovative financial and commercial focus of one of the world's top capitals, then the moral and ethical framework which undergirds it must remain a top priority. We cannot simply assume such things as quality, honesty and integrity. They need constantly to be worked at, not least when times are hard, when the going is tough, and there always lurks the temptation to cut corners and lower standards. This we simply cannot afford to do.

In the day of prosperity be joyful, and in the day of adversity consider.

People in commerce often say that the Church is always berating them for creating the wealth which, among other things, enables them to give to those who make requests of them. In response, I would say that a proper hesitation on the part of the Church is itself based on a similar hesitation in the scriptures themselves about our human nature; about what happens when human beings, left to themselves and the pursuit of their own ends, are cast off entirely from any religious and Christian understanding. When we are in pursuit of wealth and this world's goods as ends in themselves, we become so conformed to this world that it is difficult to think and conceive of anything else. Lady Judith Wilcox put it well when she posed the question in the annual lecture to the British Institute of Management in 1990 as to how far ethical codes can ever become entirely self-sufficient 'without a core of basic religious beliefs to feed and nourish them through the long winter months'. Furthermore, the scriptural writers are always reminding us about our 'condition', about our 'being'; and saying that there is within each of us, by virtue of the fact that we are human, that which tells us not so much about what we ought to do, as about who and what we are; yes, indeed, we are individuals but we are also members one of another.

We all surely recognise that left to ourselves, to our own decisions, to our own devices and desires, we shall indeed fail to do those things which we ought to do, and do those things which we ought not to do, and this will apply in our personal lives just as much as in the pursuit of our professions. In other words, there lurks in all of us that tendency to over-emphasise ourselves, to gratify our own wants, desires and expectations at the expense of the communal, when, in fact, the one must necessarily always be seen in the wider context of the other. It is here that the specifically religious and Christian language of sacrifice, self-offering and self-giving, of love and concern for one's neighbour as well as for oneself, becomes all the more relevant and necessary. As Peter Sedgwick in his book, *The Enterprise Culture*, has put it: 'A theology of enterprise is neither political nor adversarial. It is about rediscovering the dynamic of society under the creative energy of God.'

It is the business of the Church ever to remain faithful and true to the message of its founder – the words and works of Jesus; to speak them in season and out of season, ever setting before men and women that higher vocation to which we are called, the privilege of participating together in his creative purposes for us and for his world. We need to be mindful, too, that even as we pass through things temporal we do not lose sight of things eternal. At the end of the day we shall all have to render account before him from whom no creature is hidden, for, in the words of the writer of the Letter to the Hebrews, 'all are open and laid bare to the eyes of him with whom we have to do'. No wonder the writer of Ecclesiastes urges us: 'In the day of prosperity be joyful, and in the day of adversity consider.'